Restoring Sight to the Deaf Man

by Bishop Michael Scotto-Daniello

Copyright

Restoring Sight to the Deaf Man

Paperback edition

Self published with Create Space
by Bishop Michael Scotto-Daniello

First Edition March 2014
ISBN 978-0615733678

Disclaimer: Every effort was made to present the information in this book as accurately as possible at the time of the publication date. The author makes no guarantees as to the practices or policies by individual governments, political entities, people or corporations after the publication of this book.

With grateful appreciation to Deacon Stefan Weidenbach whose commitment to Christian ethics and justice inspired me to write this book.

I also wish to acknowledge the generosity of Maria Weidenbach and others who remain anonymous, whose help made this book possible. Thank you.

Table of Contents

Copyright 2

Foreword 6

A Third World Nation? 12

The New Religion 17

Distributism 26

Christian Ethics and Medical Care........................... 30

Christian Ethics and the Legal Profession.................. 43

The Media.. 54

The Danger of Secularization 65

Let Your Light Shine! 72

We the People 82

The Poor 94

Capitalism and Christianity 111

Wages 131

What Can We Do?... 137

Foreword

When I was a child, I lived on City Island in the Bronx. It was a beautiful little community with trees and friendly people. Everyone knew everyone else. Walking around the neighborhood, you certainly got the impression that this was a small town right out of New England. I often liked to go through the wooded areas on the Island. One day as I was walking through one of the wooded areas, I stumbled upon a hornet nest. It was buzzing with activity and seeing all the hornets around I kept my distance. Unfortunately, I was unable to go past the nest and I needed to do so. My fear kept me from going forward.

As I left that area, very disappointed at not being able to continue my exploration, I had a wonderful idea. I got a few of my friends together and we surveyed the area where the hornet nest was. We saw it was right next to a small pond of water. That evening, when the hornets had settled back into their comfortable little nest, we gave it a good kick right into the pond. The hornets never expected what happened to them and were unable to fight back. Needless to say, the problem was solved.

I have often looked back at that memory and kept it as a lesson for myself. It taught me that with a little thought, good advice, and courage, I was able to solve any problem that confronted me no matter how dangerous or complex.

You know, there are two types of sight. The first one is the literal sight of our eyes. It is our visual perception. The other sight is our general perception of the world around us. This is our figurative or intellectual sight. It comes to us through our knowledge and what all of our senses tell us. It is this sight that depends so much on what we hear from those around us and how we process that information.

Remember the old proverb, "the blindest man is he who refuses to see." To this I would also add the words "and listen to the world around him."

As Christians we are given all the counsels and directions we need to produce a perfect a society here on earth. Christ has shown us the way and He asks us to follow Him. He has given us this life and this test to show ourselves worthy of Heaven. What a great gift we have received from Him! So, then why do we seem to ignore not only the way to our salvation, but all of His counsels and directions as well?

Christianity is actually a necessary tool within our culture. It provides us with a value structure with which we are able to judge what is right and what is wrong. It is a safeguard against all distorted morality which will eventually lead to the decline and fall of civilization.

With all the catastrophic developments in our society today, it is with these thoughts that I now ask you: Where is Christ in Christian America? Are we ashamed of Him? Or are we merely ignorant to how we should follow Him and present Him to the world? In one sense, we cannot separate our faith from how we govern ourselves, or let ourselves be governed.

"We in America do not have government by the majority. We have government by the majority who participate." - Thomas Jefferson

If you were to say that the United States of America is a democracy...you would be wrong. The United States is now a plutonomy. It means that the wealthiest of Americans benefit from what we have to offer, to the detriment of the less fortunate. The best way to relate this would be the 1% vs. the 99%. The most definitive evidence that our democracy has died is the fact that in 2012, a recall election was held in Wisconsin. The governor's intent was to break the public employee Unions. Then, he would break the private company Unions. His ultimate goal being to stomp out worker's rights. That's kind of scary!

When he came up for the new election, he was funded by some very wealthy people who were using him to push forward their agenda regarding the demolition of worker's rights. The other candidate had only a few million dollars. The incumbent governor used his enormous amount of donations to bombard the people of Wisconsin with inaccurate, sleazy and negative campaigning against the other candidate. The other candidate was for the workers' rights. Through the use of money and the media, the incumbent was able to retake his seat. People were astonished. He did not win by a large margin, but he still won. He literally bought the election. Once again, money decided an election. It wasn't free speech or informed decision. It is more evidence of the plutonomy that has now taken over our democracy.

"The scoundrel's methods are wicked, he makes up evil schemes to destroy the poor with lies, even when the plea of the needy is just." -Isaiah 32:7

I also fault the people who did not take the time to really check out the truth in this situation. The people, through the persuasion of the media and an inaccurate understanding of each candidate, voted for the guy who wanted to hurt them. That's the fault of the people. I watched one man on a television news program start to cry stating, "Democracy is dead! It has died before our very eyes!" It was a very strong statement to be made. Unfortunately it is also an accurate one.

You can't deny it; something has gone horribly wrong with our Christian American society and our democracy in general. Most of us are totally unaware of it or we are apathetic to it or simply don't know how to effectively confront it. To be sure, our Christian faith is being replaced by general fear, apprehension, misinformation and atheistic capitalism. We need to do something before it's too late. We can already see the disastrous effect that it has had and will have upon us all. Love, true Christian love, has all but disappeared; it has been replaced by the ultimate love of self in all its monstrous forms.

Society has now succeeded in teaching us all to be selfish and to pass this distorted value on to our children. We no longer live with our Christian faith in perspective, but rather, with "get all you can right now, because this is it, ladies and gentlemen." A better description might be what I saw on a bumper sticker one day: "He who has the most toys when he dies wins!" I wouldn't call going to hell a prize! Would you?

We must make a total change in our lives. It is the only answer to our situation. Like it was with Christ, with love and the force of people united together who say no to the evils in our world. I know that as individuals, we are limited. It's like a grain of sand caught in a cog. One grain has little affect...but if the sand comes rushing in...the machine of evil will come to a grinding halt. So it is with us, there is always strength in numbers. With Christ to support us, how can we fail?

I hope that these words and ideas will raise awareness to these issues and put our fundamental Christian Gospel values into the right perspective for each of us.

The new leadership we support is that of the social Kingship of Jesus Christ. It is He, as stated by sacred scripture, which has shown us the way. We know that our true home is in Heaven. We know that this world will pass away and a new and perfect one will be created out of the ashes. We however, still have the responsibility here to make this world the best that we can. Was it not Christ Himself who told us what the greatest two commandments are? Do we live up to them? Remember that the litmus test to the morality of any society is to see how it cares for the most vulnerable of its citizens. I really don't think the US will get high marks. Do you?

"We have no government armed with power capable of contending with human passions unbridled by morality and religion. Avarice, ambition, revenge or gallantry would break the strongest cords of our Constitution as a whale goes through a net. Our Constitution is designed only for a moral and religious people. It is wholly inadequate for any other."-John Adams.

Consider this book as food for the soul. I will deal with so many issues that touch us each and every day. Any political content is only meant to be seen in the light of a Christian perspective. I give no endorsement to any political view. In fact, my view is only for Christ. So here goes.

A Third World Nation?

In August 2010, while watching the TV, I saw something that really disturbed me. There was a group of Christian young people who came in from Norway with their Pastor. They were in the Reading, Pennsylvania area and were helping a group of destitute men and women living in a shelter. They then went to a daycare facility with underprivileged children and were helping them as well. The Pastor exclaimed how lucky they were for living in Norway. They had so much abundance and good living for all. He was proud to be Norwegian. He looked down upon the failed social system in place here in America. I actually felt very ashamed and, for the first time, I began to think that maybe America was truly becoming a third world nation along with its Christian heritage disappearing.

The questions we need to ask ourselves: are we becoming a third world country and a Godless nation besides? There seems to be a growing lower class, a thinning middle class and an ever enriching, but very small, upper class. We see our Christian faith slowly but surely squeezed out of all facets of our daily lives. Money and the ways of its acquisition have become the new religious force. We now worship at the altar of materialism. It is called capitalistic atheism.

We all see this and, as a society, do nothing about it. We watch as secularism, capitalistic atheism and poverty grow before our very eyes. We have a catastrophic health care system that caters to the rich and virtually ignores the poor. We must save for our own retirements since employers have all but taken any retirement benefits away from their workers. People are being forced out of their homes through foreclosures. People are behind on their other loans as well. Even the minimum wage has its opponents who are trying to abolish it. If Jesus were to have a visible presence walking among us...what would He say?

"This is what the LORD says: Do what is just and right. Rescue from the hand of his oppressor the one who has been robbed. Do no wrong or violence to the alien, the fatherless or the widow, and do not shed innocent blood in this place." -Jeremiah 22:3

With the financial crisis that began in 2007, we saw governments give billions to big business, those who caused the problem. They gave virtually nothing to its private citizens. Our government gives huge tax breaks to the rich while the middle and lower classes are taxed to the hilt.

What social programs exist, if they haven't already been cut, to help those less fortunate to get back on their feet for a fighting chance?

On the religious front, we all say that we believe and accept Jesus. But tell me, how we show that commitment in our own lives? It seems to me that we pay lip service to God and really don't do much else to show our Christian values. Our culture has become blatantly anti-Christian.

Our Christian faith is not a one moment affirmation, but rather, a lifetime commitment of saying yes to Christ each and every moment of the day. In contrast to this, we have become selfish, hedonistic, Godless, and xenophobic. We have lost our compassion and truly lost sight of what it means to really be a Christian living in the 21st century. I am not speaking about a select few, but our society and culture as a whole.

The Bible is very specific on how we need to act and to treat our brothers and sisters here upon the earth. How many of our richer brothers and sisters in Christ ever really think about the immorality they support each and every day of their lives? Or how we enable them with our complacency?

"Suppose a man comes into your meeting wearing a gold ring and fine clothes, and a poor man in shabby clothes also comes in. If you show special attention to the man wearing fine clothes and say, 'Here's a good seat for you,' but say to the poor man, 'You stand there' or 'Sit on the floor by my feet,' have you not discriminated among yourselves and becomes judges with evil thoughts? Listen, my dear brothers: Has not God chosen those who are poor in the eyes of the world to be rich in faith and to inherit the kingdom He promised those who love Him? But you have insulted the poor. Is it not the rich who are exploiting you? Are they not the ones who are dragging you into court?"- James 2:2-6

We need to let our "light shine before men," "that they see the good that we do and give glory to God." So where has God gone in our lives? It seems that He has fallen so many places behind our new number one religion...the acquisition of wealth, more plainly put, MONEY. Or, if you like, my newest term: capitalistic atheism.

Atheism is a denial of the existence of God. It also views our lives here on earth as the only ones we have. It ignores salvation and certainly dismisses damnation. It fits in perfectly with the concept of capitalism. We know that capitalism is the ideology used to describe the unrestricted and self-centered access of wealth. Do you think that what men have done today in our culture is nothing less than capitalistic atheism?

We have set money up as our new god. It is a god of this earthly life. It provides to those who worship it, their only salvation. They seek especially through social means to gain the access for them to get more money. But tell me, what do they do with all this wealth when they die? How do they explain to Almighty God the unethical means that were used to acquire all this money? Do people think that they can bribe God? Can the rich buy their way into Heaven? I don't think so!

I am continually amazed by the four countries that have resisted the International Money Fund (IMF) and have prospered. These four are: China, Russia, Brazil, and India. Russia has now invented a new Ion Drive that is capable of long hauls in space. The Russians have announced their intentions of colonizing the moon and then going on to Mars. All this is projected to happen within the next twenty years. What do we do here in the United States?

We make the rich richer and the poor poorer with no concern whatsoever to the betterment of man and society in general. The Russians have also shown off, for public display, their new portable chapels for their armed forces. They are huge boxes except that when they open up, they become churches. They have altars inside and everything else that an Orthodox priest needs to say Mass. They are lifted and placed by helicopter. We used to make fun of Russia, they were the godless communists. Now they excel in so many things and we sit here and stagnate. Is that what we want?

Do you realize that we can greatly increase our quality of life just by implementing New and Old Testament Biblical ideas and practices in a very fundamental and simple way? The answer is that simple. Yet getting the process to kick-start is the most difficult part.

We need to truly rethink our values and what our culture means and should be for us. What are our priorities? Is it the betterment of us and mankind in general? Or is it our hedonistic pleasures, our ultimate love of self? How do we value ourselves and what we do? "He who would seek to save his life shall lose it. And he would lose his life shall save it?" Ever think that those words were really meant for us? The answer is pretty obvious and, after reading this book, I hope it will become clearer if you're not sure.

The New Religion

Think slavery in America is dead? Well, it's not. It has a new face now. It's called indentured servitude and it's all due to credit and money. The whole situation is whitewashed and presented to us as something good with a whole new set of heinous rules. We are slowly but surely being inescapably lured into financial servitude. We live for money, play for money, work for money, and sometimes put ourselves at great risk for...MONEY. But why do we do this? What has happened to us that we can see no further than our own greed? Is this Christian?

"Keep your life free from love of money, and be content with what you have; for He has said, 'I will never fail you nor forsake you.'"- Hebrews 13:5

We must remember that money in and of itself is neither good nor evil. It is the choice that we make in how we use it, or how we acquire it. Money has been around since the beginning of structured society in one form or another. Initially it was the barter system. Then it developed into the concept of currency as we know it today. What has changed is the unbridled amount of greed that has swept into our hearts and the way our culture has changed to allow for this greed to go unchecked for the advantage of the few and the harm of the many.

What we must fight now is free market capitalism. Free market capitalism basically means that if you keep markets unregulated in all arenas, business will keep itself well regulated and allow sufficient competition. This is so that a man with ingenuity and hard work can rise to the top and be a millionaire. How? By using capital at his disposal or, in reality, someone else's capital, and getting a bunch of wage slaves to produce it into goods for him while he works to manage it, until he either succeeds or fails. This happens on either a large scale or on a small scale.

The business world working on the free market model has shown itself time and time again unwilling to discipline itself and more interested in satisfying the bottom line, its profits. Greed is the name of the game. Money truly is the new god for those who espouse this ideology and practice.

If I remember correctly, the first Commandment says: "I am the Lord your God, you shall have no other gods but me." When Christ was asked what the greatest commandment was, He stated that "you shall love the Lord your God with all your heart, and mind, and soul." He stated that the second greatest commandment was to love our neighbor as we love ourselves. But do we follow these two commandments? These statements in the Bible are pretty clear cut. They are directives from God as to how we should act within society towards one another and towards God Himself. They are counsels for right living. If we exercised more charity towards one another and a lot less greed, we would be much better off individually and as a society. This lack of love and respect for God and each other translates into discord and a lack of harmony. So too, those in power act this way as well and that translates into how our politicians treat us.

"All the perplexities, confusions, and distress in America arise, not from defects in their constitution or confederation, not from want of honor or virtue, so much as from the downright ignorance of the nature of coins, credit, and circulation."-John Adams, Letter to Thomas Jefferson, August 25, 1787

Recently, I had the opportunity to visit an Occupy Philadelphia demonstration. I was struck by the sign one man held up. It stated, "I am not anti-government. The government is anti-me." I must say that I feel he was right.

"When the government fears the people, there is liberty. When the people fear the government, there is tyranny." - Thomas Jefferson

It is a well-known fact that when a government respects its people, it works to better them. The government is there to serve the people and to protect them. When people are manipulated into fearing the government, they are easier to control. The government works its way into dictatorship--a far cry from democracy. In a truly capitalist society, MONEY becomes the dictator. Those who have the finances, rule. What better way to get a society under control than to lure it with the promise of wealth and happiness of life through the acquisition of goods? It's quite simple. We are convinced into becoming a society of having rather than a society of being. We are bombarded with messages that goods bring us happiness.

Tell me, when will we learn that having generates nothing more than want and desire to simply having more and more and more? Did you ever really see someone super wealthy who is truly happy? There is no one! So money really doesn't buy you happiness. In other societies, we see the emphasis on being. The stress is on better education and for physical development. People, in this understanding, are accepting a higher obligation; it is to excel and to help humanity grow and flourish. Unfortunately, these ideals are starting to change for the worse in other countries as well. They too are tempted by the need to be self-gratified by having to the extreme.

When Jesus came to earth, He did not come by divine ambulance. He did not go right to the divine maternity wing. He did not stay in posh surroundings. Rather, He emptied Himself taking the form of a man. He was born into the world in a stable, not even a regular room. He had no heating for the cold Middle Eastern nights. The animals gave Him their breath for warmth. There were no teams of doctors around Him. He was born to what would probably be called lower middle class or even poor parents.

In fact, Jesus never lived in any form of wealth. Why did He do this? It was to give us an example of how we should live. The Lord of all kept His eyes fixed on the Kingdom of Heaven.

Jesus did state that it was harder for a camel to pass through the eye of a needle than for a rich man to enter the Kingdom of Heaven. How about when He stated that we should store up our treasure in Heaven where neither moth nor thief will deprive us of it?

It is true that we must live in this world. God has given us creation that we might have dominion over it. The problem comes in with whether or not we use creation for a good end or for a selfish one. We must use the world's resources for good. We must always try to better ourselves and the rest of humanity through the altruistic use of science and resources. It will improve the quality of life that we have now and guarantee a better future for the generations to come.

We are losing so many species of animals every year; this is all thanks to big business. Is this fair? We are custodians of God's creation. We also have the responsibility to pass it on to our children and their posterity. Anyone think that Big Industry is holding up the ethics of Gospel values?

We should develop medicines and our scientific knowledge and capacity; not for profit and material gain, but for communal gain. Tell me, how far have we come scientifically using our capitalistic atheism? Have we finished the space station? Have we gone to Mars? How about all the diseases we have still not cured? How many diseases have we cured but not allowed the treatment to become public because it is simply not financially feasible to do so? It's true, we have made some strides...but it's not as many as it should be. It's all dictated by the almighty dollar!

How ridiculous have we become, even to our own detriment, to look for "get rich quick" schemes that don't even work. Or, we are put into situations where we are put down while someone else takes advantage of us.

For example, did you ever hear the story about the American businessman who was at the pier of a small coastal Mexican village when a small boat with just one fisherman docked? Inside the small boat were several large yellow fin tuna. The American complimented the Mexican on the quality of his fish and asked how long it took to catch them.

The Mexican replied, "Only a little while." The American then asked why he didn't stay out longer and catch more fish.

The Mexican said that he had enough to support his family's immediate needs. The American then asked, "But what do you do with the rest of your time?"

The Mexican fisherman said, "I sleep late, fish a little, play with my children, take siesta with my wife, Maria, stroll into the village each evening where I sip wine and play guitar with my amigos, I have a full and busy life, señor."

The American scoffed, "I am a Harvard MBA and could help you. You should spend more time fishing and with the proceeds buy a bigger boat. With the proceeds from the bigger boat, you could buy several boats. Eventually you would have a fleet of fishing boats. Instead of selling your catch to a middleman, you would sell directly to the processor, eventually opening your own cannery. You would control the product, processing and distribution.

"You would need to leave this small coastal fishing village and move to Mexico City, then LA and eventually NYC where you will run your expanding enterprise."

The Mexican fisherman asked, "But señor, how long will this take?" To which the American replied, "15-20 years."

"But what then, señor?"

The American laughed and said that's the best part. "When the time is right you would announce an IPO and sell your company stock to the public and become very rich, you would make millions."

"Millions, señor? Then what?"

The American said, "Then you would retire. Move to a small coastal fishing village where you would sleep late, fish a little, play with your kids, take siesta with your wife, stroll to the village in the evenings where you could sip wine and play your guitar with your amigos."

Does this really make any sense? Why fix something that is not broken? The man was perfectly happy with his life the way it was. This man understood those things which truly make us happy in life and not this demonic obsession with money. Who would profit from something like this? Certainly the winner in this little story was not the hard-working man but the one who schemed (and scammed) the man so that the schemer could get richer. There was no hard work by the capitalist. I could really go on with my own lamentations as to how we have stunted ourselves by our greed. But to what purpose? The damage is already in so many other scenarios that have already been done and we must fix it.

Unfortunately, capitalism may actually have its roots with a Christian Protestant reformer in 1531. His name was John Calvin. His religious philosophy is known as Calvinism. Calvinism began measuring whether or not one was saved based on economic success. Since salvation was already predetermined by God, it has its signs here on earth. The rich man is obviously blessed by God. The essential understanding is the Old Testament Jewish theology that the blessings of God will be realized here upon earth. So, the more God loves you, the more material goods He gives you. I see a problem with that. It certainly does conflict with what Jesus told us about the Kingdom of God, "which is not of this world." Certainly, this teaching of Christ's was against the prevailing understanding of His day. Israel was not looking for a Heavenly Messiah but rather an earthly one who would lead them into battle so that they might conquer all and in so doing, realize God's ultimate favor here on earth.

If we take this Old Testament view and modernize it, we can see that in the hands of classical economists that one betters society by making as much money as he can, regardless of the human cost, and thus we now arrive at the Free Market Economy. This understanding is completely twisted against Christian understanding, ethics, and values.

Wasn't it Jesus who specifically stated that, "You cannot serve two masters"? Did He not also say in the same breath that, "you cannot serve both God and Mammon (money)"? In Matthew 6:19 and following, we have the most succinct and eloquent biblical refutation of Capitalism. Both of the previous quotes are taken from that passage.

I have always thought of a definition of personal sin as, "when you do things that set yourself up as a god." Wasn't the first sin of Adam and Eve becoming more god-like by having the knowledge of good and evil? They ate the fruit off the tree of knowledge. They were specifically told not to eat the fruit of that tree. So, in our own lives, when we set ourselves up as gods by attempting to amass as much wealth as we can, we're doing the same thing. Where does our real happiness lie? Is it on earth or in Heaven? Our actions should always reflect this question. If we want it all right now, we should not be surprised when God confirms our decision and denies us Heaven.

Distributism

In order to refute Calvin's ideas, Christian authors in the early 1900s began to rediscover and extol the concept of Distributism which was practiced at the time of Christ. This economic model was even practiced by St Joseph who was Jesus' foster father. It is the right of a man to own property by which he might take capital and produce it into goods for sale or consumption.

This model is harmonious with Christianity in that the salvation of one's soul is figured into the equation far above the right to make money. Farmers and textile producers would be the modern day remnants of this system. A Christian society did not see life as the necessity to amass wealth, but as a period to accomplish the salvation of the soul. This focus on the spiritual ends brings about a natural frugality with resources, money, and modesty in the way one spends one's time and engages in worldly goods.

The Christian author of the late 18th and early 19th century, Hillaire Belloc, said:

It has been found in practice (that is, it is discoverable through history) that economic freedom thus somewhat limited satisfies the nature of man, and at the basis of it is the control of the means of production by the family unit. For though the family exchange its surplus, or even all its production, for the surplus of others, yet it retains its freedom, so long as the social structure, made up of families similarly free, exercises its effect through customs and laws consonant to its spirit: the Guild; a jealous watch against, and destruction of, monopoly; the safeguarding of inheritance, especially the inheritance of small patrimonies. The freehold miller, in such a society as ours [English] was ours not so long ago, though he had no arable or pasture, was a free man. The yeoman, though he got his flour from the miller, was a free man. – ("An Essay on the Restoration of Property," pg. 27)

We need to speak for a moment about Guilds. They came about by those who did not wish to farm or produce textiles. Guilds were a body of craftsmen in given disciplines such as those of blacksmith, carpenter, cobbler, tailor, butcher, etc. Their purpose was to improve craftsmanship on the part of their members and to make sure that they were operating fairly. Dishonest workers would be thrown out of the Guild and as such lose business due to a bad reputation. Guilds were inherently Christian bodies, with their patron saints, celebrations, banners to process into Liturgy with, and enjoyed protection given by the Church. Its members and leaders were all craftsmen themselves employed in a given trade, not bureaucrats looking to spend the hard earned money of its workers for political gain. Always they defended the livelihood of the worker. So, stealing the means by which a man feeds his family through monopolizing and downsizing was no different than stealing the food itself from a worker's own children.

Let me make a point here that the Guilds are nothing like today's Unions. The Unions started out on the right foot and then over time many, though not all, allowed themselves to become soft and complacent with big business and industry. They used to fight for the worker's rights in the workplace. The only thing that many Unions are good at now is collecting dues.

Today, there are just a few "good" Unions out there. The Guilds exist on a more personal level. They work with the craftsmen in a sense and give structure and quality assurance to the work produced. They also form a very intimate networking source for everyone involved in the Guild. Lastly, they are sources of spiritual guidance and opportunity for each member. Normally a priest is involved in each Guild to ensure the spiritual health of all the souls involved in the Guild.

This brings us to the essence of distributism, that which the Guilds labored hard to defend. Distributism has nothing to do with government re-distribution; it merely refers to the fact of private productive property being well distributed (or diffused) amongst the people. There were no large corporations, or monopolies; simply, individuals working to better themselves and each other. By having people work together in a personal and significant manner gives each person a sense of accomplishment and real self-esteem. To illustrate this point, Belloc writes:

When so great a number of families in the state possess Private Property in a sufficient amount as to give its color to the whole, we speak of "widely distributed property". It has been found in practice, and the truth is witnessed to by the instincts in all of us, that such widely distributed property as a condition of Freedom is necessary to the normal satisfaction of human nature. In its absence general culture ultimately fails and so certainly does citizenship.—(Ibid, pg. 28)

Instead of being required to sell our labor for a wage (wage slavery) in order to survive, we ourselves become the producers and consumers of our own land on our own time. As wage slaves, we must show up to work every day or else risk the wrath of our employer. How many people would trade that to be self-sufficient?

On one side, you have life in a little cubicle, no windows, bosses who harass you all day, and the best hours of your life spent not with your spouse and children but with your obnoxious boss. While on the other hand, you have life on your terms, so long as you are willing to work hard. Which system seems more conducive to holiness and general well-being?

Christian Ethics and Medical Care

Jesus Christ gave us the Beatitudes as recorded in the New Testament. The Beatitudes are presented in a positive sense, virtues in life which will ultimately lead to reward in Heaven. He taught us the Golden Rule, "to do unto others as you would have them do unto you" (Matthew 7:12). This is in stark contrast to the capitalist version of the Golden rule which simply states, "Gold rules!"

He taught us the two greatest commandments are: "to love God, and to love your neighbor as yourself "-Matthew 22:36-40, Mark 12:28-31, Luke 10:25-28.

St. Paul taught us to respect the human body, "for our bodies are temples of the Holy Spirit"-1 Corinthians 6:19.

Jesus was the Divine Physician. He healed so many people and did it for free. All He asked for was that people change their lives and show love, kindness and charity to all others they encounter. This was truly a small price for His medical healings. He did not do it for money, but rather for love. How many doctors should take this lesson to heart? The medical profession is not just a get rich quick job; it is a vocation to help all of humanity. Anyone who tells you differently is mentally twisted in my book.

Whatever happened to doctors who made house calls? How about doctors who truly live the Hippocratic Oath? Nowadays, nothing is ever said about the Hippocratic Oath. It seems to be forgotten and thrown to the wayside.

In 2007, I read the story of a very sick young girl in California. She had leukemia. Her parents had health insurance, but the medical plan shipped this poor little girl around from hospital to hospital. They were looking for the cheapest rates they could to save money. All of a sudden, due to her illness, the young lady needed a new liver. The medical plan denied the liver transplant; this was despite the fact that this young lady was going to die without it. The doctors, not having the plan approval (the money to pay for it), refused to do the surgery. Her frantic parents fought and fought to save their baby's life by trying to raise money and fighting with the insurance company. Ironically, the approval was given for the surgery the day this little angel lost her battle to hold on to life.

Who is at fault for this? Well, at first glance, it's the insurance company. How many of us also thought the doctors as well? It's true. They all take the Oath to save life. Where were they? Their attitude was no money, no surgery. That counts as murder in my book. Once again the great god MONEY has spoken.

In the United States there are fifty million people without healthcare, according to certain sources. Many are afraid to see the doctor because they don't have the money. In fact, according to some recent statistics, eighteen thousand die every year because they do not have the proper healthcare. For the rest that have healthcare, there is always the fear of getting dropped for anything from failing to divulge a pre-existing condition, as small as it might be, to forgetting to list all treatments previously obtained.

Now, President Obama has changed this one small item, not allowing the insurance companies to penalize us for pre-existing conditions. It is still too little in my book. I wonder how long it will stay in effect after Obama leaves office.

I laugh when I hear politicians state that we have the greatest healthcare system in the world. Who is it great for? The health insurance companies? The doctors? The health providers? It is most certainly not the people here in the United States. While the Obama administration's new healthcare system will stop some of the unethical antics of the insurance companies, it does not include that crucial part called the public option. This would have not only made medical insurance available to more people, but also much more affordable. It would have been a step in the right direction making the medical system in the US more humane. How about those who are strategically dropped even with being up to date on premiums? Some of those who have been dropped have even been right in the middle of a serious medical crisis. The rule here seems to be, once again, BIG BUSINESS. How indeed is the medical system here the best in the world??

We all hear about socialized medicine. We also hear all forms of negativity against it, specifically from politicians claiming it will bankrupt America. We hear that people have to wait long periods of time before they get treatment. Well I asked people in Europe about their experiences and how they felt about our system here...

A friend in England told me that the UK healthcare system is socialized. It started right after World War II when everything was in shambles. They got it off the ground with very few problems and no one pays for healthcare. Their healthcare is very good as well. There are no waiting lists either. Imagine here in the US, being able to go to the hospital and not having to pay a dime for medical care and to receive good wholesome quality care. In fact, at the end of one's stay, there is a cashier by the door when you leave. This cashier gives—yes, gives—you money for transportation home. This is all on the government.

In speaking with the doctors themselves, they are government paid. They are well off and have no issues. Why is this not possible in America? Is there a good reason besides plain and simple greed? Certain politicians tell us that socialized medicine will falter. It will make us wait months on waiting lists. We will receive horrible care. What evidence do they have for these inaccuracies? Where is the proof? I see none. It seems to me that here in America, the very problems they accuse other systems of having are what's occurring here.

Incidentally, in 2012, the British government has begun the unthinkable and has tried to destroy the British health system by trying to force privatization. The result, it will die an ignominious death and the disease from which it will die is none other than GREED! We are also seeing the protests from the general population beginning to emerge.

Do you also realize that working ourselves to the bone for pennies on the dollar has its psychological ramifications? Have you looked at the European workforce, in Western Europe in particular? They work with less productivity and most have six weeks of vacation. Apart from how the economic crisis has hit them as well, they appear to not have the mental tiredness that we find here in America. When have you ever heard of Americans getting six weeks off for a vacation in recent memory? In fact, I have been told that almost 1/3 of Americans have not taken even one solid week off in several years. The rule of thumb here is ten days, which comes out to two weeks. How many employers discourage their employees from taking a solid two weeks? I dare say quite a few. This robbery of one's vacation also leads to health problems. We lag behind psychologically and need to drink stimulates, never mind the coffee, just to keep us going. After a while, all this stress and pressure will take its toll.

I saw an article on one of the internet news sources that had the title, "Are Americans Getting Lazy?" The article stated studies have been done that showed employers downsizing their workforces and pushing employees to the absolute limits of their productivity. How far can employees be pushed before they break? It seems to me that employers don't really care at all for the well-being of their staff. All they want is productivity at any cost. This is not very Christian. The most angering part of this article was the title. Don't you think that the title should have read, "Employers Drive Workers to Their Limits"? The very fact that they insinuated that Americans are lazy is not only insulting, it is more proof of how corporate America does not care about our health concerns whatsoever. It is a question of basic respect.

Yet another example of this blatant lack of respect for the American worker is the fact that this very same internet news source took the time to make fun of the French because they have a two hour lunch break and only work about twenty-eight hours a week. Wow! The French economy is much better than the American economy. Yes, it has some problems. Their problems, however, are not as bad as those of America. So, is the answer praising Americans for their measly thirty minute lunch break? Or, is the answer to be found in another direction?

Still speaking about respect, I am always amazed at the story of Dr Jonas Salk and the discovery of the polio vaccine. In the 1950s, polio was a great concern to the American people. A general drive was started and a campaign for every American to donate one dime each week towards research.

There was a great sigh of relief when the vaccine was finally developed. Dr Salk was instantly famous. He had an interview with Edward R Murrow, a well noted journalist, who asked him if he had the vaccine patented. Dr Salk said no. Murrow then asked him who the vaccine belonged to.

Dr Salk responded, "the American people." The people had paid for it out of their own pockets. Apparently Salk knew the value of medical resources and the right of the people to have them.

Recently, the South African Government had the same idea. HIV/AIDS is a huge problem in Africa. It affects the general population. One third of all pregnant mothers in Africa have HIV. At least 20,000 people die each month from the virus. The medicine to keep them alive IS READILY AVAILABLE. The drug companies, however, refused to let go of their profiteering. So people are left to die. The South African government took matters into its own hands and passed legislation to make generic drugs which are affordable and will save millions of lives. The drug companies found out and started their legal wrangling and threatened to stop all drug shipments whatsoever to South Africa. Unfortunately, South Africa had to back down. The drug companies won and millions of people lost their lives as a result.

Hey, the drug companies have their profit...That's what counts...doesn't it? Money is simply more important than even life itself. What surprises will happen on the Day of Judgment, do you think?

In the 1970s, under the Nixon administration, there exists to this day an infamous tape recording of Richard Nixon with John Erlichman. They were discussing the possibility of universal healthcare; Nixon was against it. The only concern expressed was for how profitable it would be for big business. The dialogue is easy enough to find online if you want to listen to it.

I was in an Emergency Room of a large hospital in my area. A woman came in who was obviously in need of emergency care. Before they did anything for her, they asked for her health insurance card. She did not have one. They walked away from her and left her there on a gurney. I really hope she didn't die as a result of not having medical insurance. Afterwards, I found out that there are States where if you have no medical insurance, they are only required to treat you, to "stabilize" you, and that's it! Where is the compassion? Where are the moral ethics? Who is following the Hippocratic Oath?

Again, I ask, do you remember the days when doctors made house calls? When you could call the doctor in the middle of the night? When being a doctor was not a job but a vocation? A doctor was kind of like a pastor or a priest. He was well respected and trusted to do the right thing to save lives and help people. Nowadays, it's just a job; a job that has become like any other. They now make their own hours, don't really care about you unless you pay them and, of course, that they don't make a medical mistake so they won't get sued by you. It's all just a sterile and cold interaction with the only advantage being for those in the medical business.

Besides the Hippocratic Oath, there must be a moral code to guide the physician in his actions. We learn as early as the Old Testament from Hebrew Scriptures the value of life. In the Book of Genesis, God said "Let us make man in our image and likeness" (Genesis 1:26). We learn that God instilled the "breath of life" in man (Genesis 2:7). Because all human beings are created according to God's image and given the breath of life, we are called to respect the dignity of each human being and to realize the immeasurable value each and every life represents.

Moses, who wrote the first five books of the Old Testament, lived before 1250 BC. God gave Moses the Ten Commandments; the one commandment which tells us how to treat life states: "Thou shalt not kill."-Exodus 20:13.

In pagan Greece, the early philosophers were concerned with the essence of life. Plato considered the soul to be trapped within the body, happily released upon death. Aristotle saw the body and soul as one unit, the soul being the "life principle" of the body.

Every physician who graduates from a medical school in the United States takes the Oath of Hippocrates, the Father of Medicine, who lived in Greece from about 450-375 BC. The middle portion of the traditional Hippocratic Oath expressly forbids abortion and euthanasia:

"I will prescribe regimens for the good of my patients according to my ability and my judgment and never do harm to anyone. To please no one will I prescribe a deadly drug nor give advice which may cause his death. Nor will I give a woman a pessary to procure abortion. But I will preserve the purity of my life and my art."

Thus the tradition of Western Christian civilization and American medicine is founded upon the Biblical ethic and the traditions of our Greco-Roman heritage. Our Declaration of Independence speaks of God our Creator and the Natural Law, "that every man has certain unalienable rights, namely, Life, Liberty and the Pursuit of happiness." Thomas Jefferson, the author of the Declaration of Independence, saw that we have freedom and dignity as human beings precisely because we are creatures of God. The US Bill of Rights guarantees the rights of every American citizen. These rights cannot be, and should never be, medically denied to anyone in need.

Another principle of medical ethics is the relationship between the doctor and the patient. Essential to this relationship is the element of trust. The patient trusts the physician to help him to make the right decision regarding his care. The physician should be compassionate, truthful, and respectful of the personal dignity of each and every human being he cares for. The doctor exists to heal the human person and fill himself with the virtue of goodness. The doctor is not here to fatten his wallet. Unfortunately, this has now become the primary concern for all physicians.

Another important principle of medical ethics is the act of helping others. It is using medical skills to do good for the sake of doing good. It refers to the traditional role of the physician as the Good Samaritan. The compassionate physician performs acts of charity, kindness, and mercy;

comes to the aid of the injured, the sick, and the dying; and relieves suffering. Natural or comfort care, the offering of food and water and the maintenance of body temperature and cleanliness for the dying elderly patient are forms of beneficence; as well as comforting the patient through a loving presence, palliation and prayer.

Jesus gave us the Parable of the Good Samaritan, as recorded in the Gospel of Luke:

Jesus replied, "A man was going down from Jerusalem to Jericho, and he fell among robbers, who stripped him and beat him, and departed, leaving him half dead. Now by chance a priest was going down that road; and when he saw him he passed by on the other side. So likewise a Levite, when he came to the place and saw him, passed by on the other side.

But a Samaritan, as he journeyed, came to where he was; and when he saw him, he had compassion, and went to him and bound up his wounds, pouring on oil and wine; then he set him on his own beast and brought him to an inn, and took care of him. And the next day he took out two denarii and gave them to the innkeeper, saying, `Take care of him; and whatever more you spend, I will repay you when I come back.'

Which of these three, do you think, proved neighbor to the man who fell among the robbers?" He said, "The one who showed mercy on him." And Jesus said to him, "Go and do likewise."-Luke 10:29-37

The doctor must respect the rights and dignity of each human being. The physician must be fair to his patient, respect his rights as a person, and, in true Christian Charity, must give the patient proper access to healthcare.

Finally, the doctor must be diligent to develop a virtuous character and exhibit moral integrity. We have the best role model—the great Physician, namely, Jesus Christ!

In contrast to the above description which outlines the ideal for all doctors, we have those who work in the medical industry trying to make it rich any way that they can. For example, one of the greatest blasphemies of our capitalistic and atheistic age is the so-called applied patent (like a copyright) for the maps of a living cell's genetic links. How can a company patent that which was created by God? Simply because they discover it does not mean that they own it. Once again I prove my point about capitalistic atheism running rampant throughout our culture. This is indeed more evidence that man has forgotten about God. More proof about the position of the almighty dollar.

We have become a culture that decides on who lives and who dies. There is abortion and euthanasia. The rights of the unborn are to be absolutely the same as the born. Similarly, no one has the right to decide when someone who is older or diseased is beyond their usefulness. That fact is that we are all of infinite worth before Almighty God. He has numbered the hairs upon our heads. It is His Love which holds us in existence. It will be His Love which also finally calls us forth from this life. Both acts of man clearly display the depravity of our age and demonstrate yet another facet of how our culture has become degraded. The problem then becomes one of how we value life. Do we then create classes of throw away people? Has life become that meaningless to us all? The only remedy is to bring God back into the equation of our lives.

Christian Ethics and the Legal Profession

Do you remember the legal firm in New York during 2010 that threw a Halloween Party? The boss of the firm asked all his workers to come in dressed up as the people that they had helped the banks foreclose upon. They had a good laugh all day at that party. They portrayed their victims as homeless and the lowest of the low. They made fun of them. What mercy did they show to their victims? Was there ever a mention at that firm of the predatory lending practices of the bank? What interest did they have in morality or true Godly justice?

"Beware of the teachers of the law [. . .] They devour your widows' houses [. . .] Such men will be punished severely."-Luke 20:46-47

The legal profession has been around for as long as society has kept a system of rules to keep us from anarchy. In 39BC, the philosopher Cicero stated, "The welfare of the people is the ultimate law." We must always keep in mind that only the proper and righteous laws of men are necessary to help and protect us. In a perfect system, they will always operate in congruity with God's laws and help us to lead righteous and productive lives. Such a system would facilitate the Kingdom of Heaven to manifest itself here on earth. From this, we arrive at the concept of earthly justice and its application to society.

For the Christian, the role of the attorney is like that of the doctor in that it is a vocation, a life calling. We often see attorneys today practicing their profession for financial gain and not out of love for the law and justice. Such was the problem in Jesus' day as well.

"(They) have grown fat and sleek. Their evil deeds have no limit; they do not plead the case of the fatherless to win it, they do not defend the rights of the poor." -Jeremiah 5:28

The prophet Jeremiah here speaks of the corruption that already existed in the legal profession in his day. How many attorneys do you know who will refuse a case, not out of injustice, but rather, because there is not enough money to be had? Justice has a new name. It is called MONEY !

"Do not exploit the poor because they are poor and do not crush the needy in court."-Proverbs 22:22

How many innocent people go undefended simply because they do not have enough money to afford a decent attorney? The Bible describes such men who would deny the poor as indeed evil.

"Learn to do right! Seek justice, encourage the oppressed. Defend the cause of the fatherless, plead the case of the widow." -Isaiah 1:17

Here the prophet Isaiah reproves those in the legal profession against their evildoing. He, like Jeremiah, had experienced the moral depravity of those in the legal profession. If justice does not exist in the legal profession, what then are we to say about judges and politicians?

Normally, it is from the legal profession that they come into their new positions of power.

"Do not deny justice to your poor people in their lawsuits."-Exodus 23:6

We must begin from the bottom up. We need to re-educate those who practice law and demand that they make a choice for the good of society and not their own wallets. We must demand that laws which do not protect society as a whole, or only favor the wealthy, must be abolished. We must then demand from our politicians that the procedures for electioneering be changed. It is absurd that a politician not identify with the common folk. It was in the lack of identification with the common man that most kings lost their thrones. Shouldn't we do the same here?

"The scoundrel's methods are wicked; he makes up evil schemes to destroy the poor with lies, even when the plea of the needy is just." -Isaiah 32:7

We have the tools in front of us to make government truly democratic and truly just for all. What we don't want to do is forget the lessons of the French Revolution. In that scenario, the people did nothing as they watched their liberties be stripped from them one by one. Eventually it evolved from a monarchy to a plutonomy, which is what is happening to us. The people finally exploded; they became violent and much blood was spilled. There were as many as 1500 people per week that met with the guillotine.

France became steeped in a pool of blood that knew no satisfaction. We must remember that active voice and peaceful demonstration is the way to change. The old secular proverb, as I recall it, is "the people united can never be defeated."

"Woe to those who enact evil statutes, and to those who continually record unjust decisions, so as to deprive the needy of justice, and rob the poor of My people of their rights [...] Now what will you do in the day of punishment, and in the devastation which will come from afar?" -Isaiah 10:1-3

When an employee wishes a raise, the act must come from his or her employer. So, I ask, why should politicians enact a raise for themselves? Do not politicians work for the people? Aren't we rightfully the ones who should determine the wages and benefits of our government officials?

I found a list of what certain public officials make when they retire. Here are the figures:

-The President of the United States makes 450K for life.

-The US House and Senate Members make 174K for life.

-The US Speaker of the House makes 223K for life.

-The US Majority/Minority Leaders make 194K for life.

These figures do not include the other numerous benefits that they receive, such as healthcare, for the rest of their lives. There are also no thresholds for their pensions to vest. They can serve just one measly term and are guaranteed their humungous "retirement checks and benefits" for life. How many of us have to wait five or ten years for our pensions to vest? We don't get handouts like these rich guys. WOW! The politicians certainly know how to take care of themselves. They should start learning how to take care of us! Isn't that why we voted them in?

What also gets me is that a soldier fighting in Afghanistan only makes 38K a year while on duty. Soldiers risk their very lives for us! When he or she leaves the army, he or she doesn't continue to receive this salary. The other figure is for our Senior Citizens on Social Security. They only make 12K a year. One can see how easily they could fall below the poverty level. Perhaps the politicians should ask the 1% and the corporations to pay up what they really owe in taxes and help our dear soldiers and seniors to make it through their great struggles. After all, we exist in society to help each other and not to play the predator. This is certainly not a Christian value. If you are looking to be a predator and get all the money you can, you are certainly not following the teachings of Christ.

I recently heard a great story regarding a politician who died and went before St Peter at the Pearly Gates. St Peter said to him, "My son, you have two options to choose from. You can make the choice of whether you go to heaven or hell." The politician was amazed and happily said, "My choice, HUH? OK!" St Peter than asked the man which he wished to see first. The man told him to let him see hell first. So, in an elevator he went and when it opened he was amazed. He saw in hell his country club and all his friends sipping drinks served by scantily clad waitresses and then his buddies playing a round of golf. He got back in the elevator and went up to heaven. There he saw the angels and saints all singing the praises of God in total bliss. The politician went back to St Peter who then asked him if he had made a choice. The politician then told him he liked what he saw in hell and wanted to go there. St Peter was dismayed and somewhat taken back by the comment. But he said OK to the politician and let him have his choice. The politician smiled and got into the elevator. When the elevator doors opened, a huge wall of flames engulfed the inside of the elevator and it singed his clothes. He looked out and saw desolation. People were crawling and screaming, being constantly burned, and the demons taking delight in taunting the damned souls. The devil approached the politician who was speechless. He looked at the devil and said, "This is not what I saw when I came down before!" The devil responded, "Ah! Yes! We were in campaign mode when you were first here!"

We have all been disappointed by politicians. What can we do to make the system better? I think we should totally revamp the political system. Perhaps we need three parties instead of two. We need to also change the process for electioneering so that not only the 1%, or those heavily sponsored by them, can get into office.

Once in office, we need to put in a system that provides transparency. We need to stop any "gift giving" that is going on. We need to stop lobbyists. We also need to stop any little deals that unduly influence political decisions against the will of the general public. If we do nothing, we are endorsing the political system with which we are so dissatisfied. We cannot sit back. We have to be active. Democracy requires action from the people. We are the lifeblood of our political system. Our greatest enemy is apathy.

How many of us remember the story of the Boston Tea Party? We all learned about it in grammar school. Old King George in England decided to oppressively tax the citizens of the US colonies with a Tea Tax. The Tea Tax was high and mandatory. King George decided to also send us the worst quality tea that existed. It was so bad that many colonists thought that it partly consisted of dried cow compost. In England, George's direct subjects paid a lot less tax and got the best quality. The Americans complained of how they were being taxed without any voice. It was called taxation without representation. It is a common theme that we still have to this very day. The very thing we fought against is what we have imposed upon ourselves by our own government. Funny, those who are not taxed have all the voice while we poor slobs have no voice whatsoever. Remember, it's not called a democracy; it's called a plutonomy. Unfortunately, if this trend continues along this path, it will eventually be called a dictatorship.

Another interesting rouse is the coining of a phrase by politicians who call the 1% the "job creators." It is just another unsubstantiated and worthless sound byte. First of all, how many tax cuts do these people get? And they still aren't creating jobs. They have received these special tax cuts for years and things get worse, not better. Let's look at the reasons why:

The people who are ultimately responsible for creating jobs are the 99%. The majority of us have the power. We are the ones who spend money and buy goods and services. We are the ones who move the economy. It is simple logic to assume that without money, there is no demand for goods and services in our capitalistic society. With demand, production increases and so does manufacturing and, thus, yes you guessed it, jobs. The 1% does not spend its money. They are too busy making more money by squeezing the labor force to its limits and not hiring, unless there is a greater demand. This is why Iceland, for example, spent its bailout money on the people in general. Look how fast they got back on their feet. The phrase "job creators" is nothing more than another disguised way of saying, "ALMS FOR THE RICH! ALMS FOR THE RICH!"

Another part of the legal profession are those who enforce the laws. To this category we place the police and the military. The role of a policeman is to serve and to protect. The crucial question becomes whom do they serve and protect within our society? Are they the security guards for the 1%? Such immorality can be plainly seen in how the police have brutalized without provocation those within the OCCUPY Movement. How many times have we seen the police use undue or excessive force? I once heard the mayor of New York in an interview against the OCCUPY Movement call the NY Police Department "his army." These are truly disturbing words indeed. Perhaps the motto of the police should be, "To subjugate and to bully." It does seem more appropriate.

I recall the story of a neighbor in a small town who saw some light in his huge shed. He went out to investigate and saw two burglars gathering his stuff to steal. He called the police and they unemotionally told him that they could not respond at that moment. They told him to go back into the house and lock the door. He hung up the phone mad at the lack of care the police showed in the situation. He waited thirty seconds and then called back the police and told them he had shot the two burglars. The police hung up and within three minutes there were five police cars at the property along with an emergency services van and an ambulance. They apprehended the burglars and in a quizzical way a policeman asked the man, "I thought you said you shot them?" The man replied, "I thought you had no one to respond."

Into this category of the legal profession, I also place the immigration authorities. I am waiting for the day when they decide that it is more cost effective to go after our senior citizens rather than illegal immigrants who break the law. Why? Well, if they round up senior citizens and get them out of the country, the government saves on Social Security and Medicare payments. Besides, they don't run fast and it's easier to catch them instead. The poor dears usually don't remember how to get home anyway. The way our government is going, I wouldn't put it past them to implement this travesty of justice either.

Law enforcement cannot morally hide behind their badges in order to enforce the rights of the 1%. I remember the trials at Nuremberg after World War II in which the Nazi soldiers defended themselves by saying, "I was only acting upon the orders I was given." They were convicted just the same. We still have the obligation as Christians to follow our rightly formed consciences and do what is right before the eyes of the Lord.

As an example of what Law Enforcement should do, consider a foreclosure case in Georgia. A bank foreclosed on the house of a 103 year old woman (almost 104) and her 83 year old daughter. When the Sheriff came and saw the two women, he immediately knew that making both homeless would have killed the 103 year old woman pretty quickly. Her daughter was not in much better shape either. They had been living in the house for 53 years. It appears that they might have taken out a home equity loan on the house to catch up on some bills that needed to be paid. The Sheriff refused to evict them. There was a moving company as well that was hired by the bank, and they too refused to do anything. Because the Sheriff relented, the bank backed off to rethink the entire operation. This Sheriff stands as a shining example that the motto "To Serve and Protect" means to carry out true Christian morality and justice. Let's hope more officials will get the point as well.

It's amazing how fast law enforcement is to help foreclosures happen. Where are the politicians, for example, to stop and punish the predatory lending practices of the banks? How about stopping the travesty of bungled foreclosures where the bank has all the cards (most of them illegal and unethical) and the homeowner is lead to the slaughter?

"I believe that banking institutions are more dangerous to our liberties than standing armies. If the American people ever allow private banks to control the issue of their currency, first by inflation, then by deflation, the banks and corporations that will grow up around [the banks] will deprive the people of all property until their children wake-up homeless on the continent their fathers conquered. The issuing power should be taken from the banks and restored to the people, to whom it properly belongs." -Thomas Jefferson

The Media

I recently had the pleasure of watching some Wonder Woman episodes from 1978/1979. They were wonderful. Wonder Woman is akin to a modern day saint in many respects. She is selfless. She fights for true freedom; real justice and truth. Marvel comics truly created a wonderful role model in her.

What's more interesting about her are the stories that were presented in the series. For the second season of the series, she was modernized and set into life in the late 1970s. She fought corrupt business people as her specialty. She stressed the need for true democracy, real transparency in our society's leaders, and the genuine need for real peace and love among all humanity. What are the themes in today's shows? Do we see these concepts in any of our shows today? A change has taken place just within a few decades.

What we watch on TV has a definite impact upon us. TV will shape our views and even convince us into certain ways of thinking. Unfortunately, these trends are bringing us more and more into the un-Christian society we have today where everything is a competition and all about "dog-eat-dog." We laugh at the losers for being defeated and we applaud the winners for clawing their way ruthlessly to the top. These reality shows instill the illusion that we also can be rich and famous. We are taught that this is the true meaning of success. Isn't true success living as Christ wanted us to live? How about loving our neighbor? How about showing genuine charity? Do reality shows want to instill a new set of values in us?

Forget about all those ridiculous reality shows for a moment, what values do shows like the Sopranos teach us? To be a bunch of psychopaths who rob, kill, hurt, and steal all in the name of getting more money? Is this what we are to look up to? Is this the Christian way?

We are being taught that the greatness of creation is all here and not in Heaven. We are being convinced that the need to have, to possess, to own, is tantamount and essential to any form of happiness. We are devolving socially into little selfish animals that look blindly at today and can see no further. A secular proverb that is appropriate here is that the blindest people are those who refuse to see. The wool is being pulled right over our eyes and we simply do not see it.

The media is a very passive weapon. It shapes our opinions and teaches us its own twisted version of what is wrong and right. People listen to the media. It exposes us to new ideas and ideologies and tells us that they are what we should follow. Tell me, when you see a story on TV, don't you tend to believe it? The media is not impartial or fair. It pushes its own agenda and shapes minds to lead us all into the directions and approvals of those behind the media. The agenda is Capitalism. Ever notice how those in the media tend to glorify the wealthy? Heroes are not heroic unless they have lots of money. Every show or news piece ultimately centers on money and its acquisition or loss.

The wealthy are always portrayed as some kind of gods. Besides having a lot of money, what have the rich really done to be heroes? They have no great virtues or intellect. They do not help mankind; they rob from us. Why are we supposed to care about them and put them on pedestals?

Another example is a new electronic game that is out on the market. Yes, there are tons of evil, violent, immoral games out there, but a new one has introduced itself that makes fun of the housing crisis. The player of the game is directed to "kill" all the homeless people he can find to win. How sick is this? What kind of parent would allow any of these games? They become the perfect brainwashing tool for the young to make good little capitalistic atheists out of them.

How about the internet? There has been a push recently to censor it. Certain businesses are stating that copyright infringement is rampant on the internet. At present, there is no reason, other than monetary gain, to censor the digital highway. For example, music companies have pulled in record profits for music being downloaded according to certain consumer groups. There is no justification for what they assert. The true motive once again appears to be GREED!

It's amazing how a free and unrestricted internet actually aids in so many things such as freedom of speech and expression. To hinder it for the sake of profit by the very few is clearly, once again, a violation of civil rights and civil liberties. All one would have to do is copyright whatever he or she pleased to stifle all postings out there on a particular subject. We will once again be robbed into silence!

The final aspect of the media that I want to speak about is the news media. Journalists have a great responsibility in getting information out to the public. In a perfect system, their job is to get at the truth and to present it in a clear, concise and unbiased manner. We are not in a perfect system. What journalists should be doing is standing outside the cycle of corruption and manipulated information that makes up the power relations of society. They can show audiences the truth of the system and how it works.

We also need to have transparency with our journalists. They need to prove that they are not manipulating the news for their own ends or for those corporations that own them. We must not allow them to manipulate the TV and other forms of mass media to shape public opinion. This too can be considered a form of brainwashing.

One potential antidote to this subversion of journalistic integrity is an independent news media organization with the courage and the guts to expose the system to the light of day; so that the force of public opinion, shame, and law can bring about a correction.

Unfortunately, as already said, it turns out that most of the news agencies with the power to do this are themselves both owned and controlled by other players in the system.

TV news programs are owned by the same massive corporations that exert control over much of the rest of economy and culture. TV news people manipulate information in such a way that is designed to attract audiences and to push their own political agendas. They also aggrandize themselves so they will appear as heroes and celebrities before the public.

Of course, the news media does reveal a certain amount of truth to save face. Such practices are more dangerous to the public because stories that can be somewhat verified can also be twisted and manipulated into something totally different in order to push an agenda.

I found it interesting that in 2012, a prestigious University in New Jersey did research on the news media in general. Their results were eye-opening. Apparently the news agency out there that caters to the 1% was considered the worst in presenting. It did not cover many important stories. It pushed its pro-capitalist agenda feigning actual news stories and it left those viewers who exclusively watch it ignorant to the world and its daily events. The university researchers went on to say that there was a news show on one of the comedy channels that actually gave a fuller picture of each day's events, as well as leaving people who watched it better informed.

We should not put all our faith and trust in a news program just because it constantly waves the flag and says, "God bless America!" Isn't it true that the devil often appears to us as an angel of light? Deception is one of the devil's most basic strategies.

To put it plainly, the problem is that the news agencies are corporate owned. How fair or impartial can they possibly be? They are the ones who decide which news articles get published and which do not. They also decide how the news that is presented will be told.

Two college seniors wanted to try an experiment in their sociology class. They took two students, one of whom was extremely bright and one who was rather slow. They then put them in the front of the room along with the teacher. The young men then divided their class into three groups. The first group nearest the door was told that they would be asked a very difficult question. In order to help them, they could choose either the teacher or one of the two other classmates. If they got the answer right, they would get $5 each. Naturally the group chose the teacher to help them.

Then the two young men took the second group in the middle of the class and told them that they were going to be asked the same question. This time they were also told that the "slow" student had the answer written down on a piece of paper in his hand. At this the first group began to protest. The second group took no time in choosing the "slow" student to help them.

To the last group which was nearest the window, the two young men confessed that they had actually lied to the second group and that the paper with the answer on it had been given to the bright student. To prove the allegation the slow student showed that his hands were empty. The bright student also showed his hands. One of them held the actual paper with the answer written on it.

Out of the three groups, the last one got the answer right and each won $5. This was all amidst the protests from the other two groups. The teacher asked them what they wanted to prove with this little demonstration. The two young men told the teacher that there is no freedom without the truth. The first two groups were not correctly informed regarding all the facts. They were free to choose, but failed in their choices. It wasn't really a free choice because without all the facts, they were really blind in making their choices and in their understanding of the events around them. Aren't all of us in this very same situation when it comes to the news?

Can you deny that the media is a powerful tool in the proper shaping of society? The media influences our thinking on a very profound level. It gives us projected experiences and views which we become accustomed to and, therefore, begin to accept as the way things should be. The problem is determining if the news, for example, presents to us fair and impartial investigative reporting.

The media can also be a powerful tool for a government to shape the ideas and attitudes of all its citizens. It can be used to educate and enlighten. It can also be used to instill fear in people so that they become more mentally pliable and easier to control. Fear mongering seems to be all the rage today in the media. Fear can be used as a tool to intimidate and mislead people into bad choices.

It's important to discuss the idea of fear for a moment. Fear can be good or bad. Healthy fear teaches us respect and helps us to do what is right. For example, there is fear of the Lord. This is definitely spoken of several times in the Bible. It is a healthy respect.

There is another type of fear mentioned in the Bible which is not beneficial to us. This is "emotional fear" mentioned in 2 Timothy 1:7: "For God has not given us a spirit of fear, but of power and of love and of a sound mind."

It is true that sometimes we are afraid. This "emotional fear" overcomes us, and to overcome it, we need to trust in and love God completely. "There is no fear in love. But perfect love drives out fear, because fear has to do with punishment. The one who fears is not made perfect in love" (1 John 4:18). It is God Himself who constantly reminds us to "fear not." As Christians, we are told to not be afraid by Christ Himself. With God as our Father, we will always be loved. We should not put stock into anything that the media tells us. We should not be led to fear in order to be intimidated by the government.

"The man who reads nothing at all is better educated than the man who reads nothing but newspapers."-Thomas Jefferson

I myself don't read newspapers anymore. Nor do I watch news shows for anything that is beyond the weather segment. It seems like a total waste of time to put any faith into what we are being told. In fact, judging from what is happening with the news media, it seems that they are mostly fear mongering anyway. Keep the American people fearful, apprehensive and in debt and America's citizens become easy to manipulate and control.

So, now, what should we do to correct this wrong? The greatest challenge to insure the impartiality of fairness of the news media is to force accountability upon it. This accountability is the first step in wisdom. We need to have a watchdog that monitors the media. This watchdog should also have the ability to enforce censure and sanctions upon those news agencies which consistently run stories that show a particular agenda. Such a group would have as its end the instilling of responsibility upon the news media to ensure that it remains fair and impartial. Such a watchdog would have to come from a fair and impartial government that would be concerned for the interests of its entire people and not just the 1%.

On TV the other day, I saw a little advert for starting younger children onto financial success. I remember when we used to teach little children their prayers and to instill in them what is right and what is wrong. See how money has become the new god? TV slowly spreads its blasphemous poison. It was done in such a way that it would not be noticed until everyone started to snare themselves into it. I really feel that the media, along with the capitalism agenda, has destroyed the family. On TV we are exposed to single parent families, divorces, dysfunctional families, promiscuity, abortion, violence, cruelty, murder, and a whole host of additional immoralities. The media exposes us to these things every day and we become used to them. We start to accept them as the norm because we are bombarded with them. This is how we are changed. Every once in a while a show with values is presented in the midst of all the dirt and we are placated. This is not the way to go.

Of all places, Italy, over the past several years, had started an anti-mafia initiative. It started in Sicily with the deaths of several judges and a priest who fought against the mafia. They were heroic in their actions. They became true martyrs in every sense of the word.

People began to push the media against organized crime through initiatives aimed at undermining the stranglehold of organized crime. People began to really see that such people are simply sick psychopaths that need to be stood up to. AND IT WORKED!!!

The government quickly followed suit and the movement grew and grew into something huge. So much of the organized crime in Italy has now been put out of business. We can move mountains if we just stand up for ourselves and for our faith!*

The last point that I wanted to make is how anti-Christian the media has become. We see other religious groups immediately standing up and resisting anything that puts them in a bad light. We as Christians must do the same.

Christianity is a religion of peace but this does not mean that we must act as sheep being led to the slaughter for a less than holy cause. We can commit as much of a sin by not doing anything as we can by doing something wrong. This is called a sin of omission.

If we truly believe that Christ is the King of kings, then we must stand up and be counted. What the media does is simply an act of bullying against us. If we do not stop it, it will continue to grow and grow. We will also lose all of our credibility before the world and we will be cast aside and stepped on all the time.

We need to see that what is happening in America truly is the work of the devil. People need to wake up and start to rectify this distortion away from God; first within themselves, and then within their families. It can be done!

The Danger of Secularization

The secret to retaking our society back from the financial terrorists is to show people that our culture is the most important element of our society; then the government and other institutions. We must take a look at where we are going. How will things end up for us? Is this what we want? Most importantly, are we in congruity with the Gospel message? Are we the lights of Christ upon the earth?

I recently read a survey in which people were asked about their church habits and their shopping habits among other things. If Americans go to church, it's for about an hour each week. When asked about shopping, Americans shop for at least five hours each week. We are brainwashed into using shopping as a form of therapy to make us feel better. We have turned ourselves into a culture of "having." This is consumerism. It comes as a result of capitalism. Ultimately, capitalism is what pulls us away from God.

How did we get this way? It seems that this radical reorientation of man's conscience began in the late 17th and early 18th century. It started with the new philosophical concept of relativism. We are now taught that each one of us has our own "truth" inside. We cannot trust that which is outside of ourselves. So, we develop a pluralism of truth. That is, each person accepting their own ideas and concepts for the good of self.

According to this concept of relativism, if someone tells me that the sky is green with yellow polka dots, I have to respect this observation. There no longer exists any objective truth. This concept is opposed to Christianity in every aspect of its ideology. It also allows for the eventual hedonistic capitalism that took root as a result. Let's face it. We have a fallen nature due to our first parents. Greed and avarice are part of our natures. Any justification to allow these characteristics of our fallen nature can, and has been, packaged for a very attractive sales pitch to one and all. Look how many people have already bought into this most heinous concept.

The other fact to be reckoned with is that any society that espouses consumerism and capitalism as its foundations is bound to eventually fall. The goods of the earth are limited. This planet is it for us right now. The goals of profitability have actually hindered us from exploring space more seriously. Right now, space exploration is not capitalistically feasible. It is way too expensive and the goals of financial reward are just too remote for now. This stands as a proof that capitalists do not look to the long term future...even for their own good.

"We should have no more use or regard for money in any of its forms than we have for dust. Those who think it is worth more, or who are greedy for it, expose themselves to the danger of being deceived by the Devil."-St. Francis of Assisi

It is important for us to build a society based upon Christian values that are both without compromise yet speak to the modern world. Such a society would devote itself to the betterment of man. Such a society would already be out in space and would also have found cures for some of the diseases that still elude treatment for us right now. Making money should not be our primary goal and we certainly should not let our finances interfere or compromise our integrity as Christians. Our first goal should always be to seek the will of God in our lives, especially through His commandments, and then to put it into practice. Then we should love and serve others. There is nothing wrong with working hard and taking pride in our work. Similarly, if we have a service or product that we can sell, that's still OK. Distributism is what man practiced during Biblical times and through the Middle Ages.

As Christians, we must also be sure to not refuse those who truly cannot pay. Especially if the good or service is something more fundamental to the general quality of life. Charity has always been a great virtue that Jesus extolled us to practice. We must always ask ourselves in all that we do, how this will serve both God and the common good of our fellow men? The book of Leviticus is quite clear on this:

"Now in case a countryman of yours becomes poor and his means with regard to you falter, then you are to sustain him, like a stranger or a sojourner that he may live with you. Do not take usurious interest from him, but revere your God, that your countryman may live with you. You shall not give him your silver at interest, nor your food for gain."-Leviticus 25:35-37

This concept is not hard to implement. It may, at first, appear difficult, but it will become contagious...a good contagious. I have always felt that good begets good...just as evil can beget evil.

However, I doubt anyone in the US could be justifiably proud that we allow our fellow citizens to literally live on the streets and die of exposure and/or starvation. In that respect, we are inhumane; Europeans think we're insane for allowing it to persist in what is arguably the richest country in the world. Of course, the rich and powerful, who stand to gain from tax rates lower than those in Europe and lower than US tax rates from the 1960s, have succeeded in flattening the US tax structure. What used to be a fairly progressive structure (high earners paid a higher percentage) has moved incrementally toward a regressive structure (low earners pay a higher percentage when various penalties are factored in, such as the inability to exploit tax loopholes for not having enough money, or Social Security taxes on all of one's income instead of the first 84K, or even sin taxes on alcohol and cigarettes).

The flabbergasting thing to me is that the poor have been convinced that the possibility of hitting it big (winning the lottery or being a pop star, an athlete, etc.), which only happens to a miniscule number of people, makes protecting immense wealth advantageous to them even when they don't have it. Hope is kept alive — and the underclass fooled with it.

Those who have less are conditioned to react to keep themselves down with no realistic way of ever getting to the top.

I want to return for a moment to the sociology class that I had spoken of earlier. A young lady who is very sympathetic with the OCCUPY Movement presented the following demonstration to her class: She brought with her a pet hamster along with some cheese and several pieces of bread. She told the class that, as we all would have guessed, the hamster's favorite food is indeed cheese. First she placed some cheese on a tabletop and covered it with a bell glass. To the side, outside the glass, she placed several pieces of bread. She let the hamster loose on the tabletop and he made a beeline right for the cheese. He struggled very hard and in vain to get the cheese. When the hamster finally gave up after such a valiant try, he ate the bread.

The young lady tried some other experiments as well which ended up as always having the poor hamster settle for the bread. Finally the young lady put out a piece of cheese and a piece of bread on the table near each other. She let the hamster go and, guess what, he went for the bread even though he saw the cheese as well. He actually settled for the bread despite seeing the cheese.

The young lady explained that, like the hamster, society has conditioned us into keeping our places. Some of us were meant to have the cheese; the rest of us are taught to settle for the bread. What a wonderful example of societal brainwashing.

The range from top to bottom of the socioeconomic scale has been widening for fifty years in the US. In Europe, except for a few royal and aristocratic families, it's been narrowing. Only recently has this started to change and skew more towards the American model.

I want to also call to mind the difference in which Christian countries celebrate Christmas. Here in the US it is, mainly, a time of gift giving. We spend our money to get those material goods to make our loved ones happy. In many Latin countries, the custom is to celebrate Christmas as a religious feast and to celebrate the gift giving on January 6. That is, the feast of the Epiphany, when the three wise men came to honor Jesus with their gifts of gold, frankincense and myrrh. I really feel that this is a better option to keep Christmas Christ-centered, which is what it should be. It is the birth of our Savior, the miracle of the God/man, who came to earth in the virgin's womb.

The time is now to make the world a better place. The time is now to enthrone Christ in our hearts and minds and to reshape our culture and society back to good and proper moral values. Step by step we would eventually make strides to bring this world back to sanity. We owe this obligation to our children and our children's children.

In doing so, we become the heroes of our age who will be remembered as the saints who made a difference and brought change and peace along with true prosperity to our planet. If we do not do this, we will go down in infamy remembered as those who let the greed, materialism and relativism of the age overwhelm us. Worse still, how will we account for ourselves before Almighty God? What excuses will we give Him? He was the One who gave us His only Son to preach the good news and show us the true way to salvation. It's never too late to start; as long as we walk this earth, there will always be HOPE!

Let Your Light Shine!

One early Saturday morning, I listened to a preacher on the radio as I ate breakfast. During her discourse, she told the radio audience that it doesn't matter what choices we make, what matters is our faithfulness to God. Even the radio show host asked her to repeat what she had said. Sure enough, she stated the same thing over again. I was astonished! Well it confirmed that I wasn't asleep either.

I thought about what she had said and then thought about someone who had the flu. The patient tells the doctor that she believes in the medicine and that it will cure her. She then decides not to take the medicine and dies as a result. The woman was definitely not too swift. She believed in the medicine, but did nothing to incorporate it into her being. If she had acted upon her knowledge and belief, she would have saved her life.

This, too, is important for all of us to remember. It is essential that we are faithful to God. It is also essential that in our continual "yes" to Him, we ACT upon His words.

"What good is it, my brothers, if a man claims to have faith but has no deeds? Can such faith save him? Suppose a brother or sister is without clothes and daily food. If one of you says to him, 'Go, I wish you well; keep warm and well fed,' but does nothing about his physical needs, what good is it?"-James 2:14-16

These words are a call to action for each one of us. We must take them to heart. If we do not, our society will never change and our culture will continue to die of its present diseases.

We also need to look at our religious leaders and what they are doing. It seems that many leaders have gone astray.

"Now a bishop must be above reproach, the husband of one wife, temperate, sensible, dignified, and hospitable, an apt teacher, no drunkard, not violent but gentle, not quarrelsome, and no lover of money." -1 Timothy 3:2-3

The last part of this quote is the one that most church people struggle with. We all need money to survive. It is true. The sin comes in when we start to build financial empires. Why do we need financial empires? Do we not become hypocrites and betray the very words and counsels of Christ? We must teach by our examples. This way is definitely more powerful and convincing than simply words.

In a letter that St Paul wrote to Timothy regarding the correct life for those in the ministry, we have the following words:

"This is what you are to teach the brothers to believe and persuade them to do. Anyone who teaches anything different, and does not keep to the sound teaching which is that of our Lord Jesus Christ, the doctrine which is in accordance with true religion, is simply ignorant and must be full of self-conceit – with a craze for questioning everything and arguing about words. All that can come of this is jealousy, contention, abuse and wicked mistrust of one another; and unending disputes by people who are neither rational nor informed and imagine that religion is a way of making a profit.

"Religion, of course, can bring large profits, but only to those who are content with what they have. I am speaking about spiritual profit here. We brought nothing into the world, and we can take nothing out of it; but as long as we have food and clothing, let us be content with that. People who long to be rich are a prey to temptation; they get trapped into all sorts of foolish and dangerous ambitions which eventually plunge them into ruin and destruction. 'The love of money is the root of all evils' and there are some who, pursuing it, have wandered away from the faith, and so given their souls any number of fatal wounds. But, as a man dedicated to God, you must avoid all that. You must aim to be saintly and religious, filled with faith and love, patient and gentle. Fight the good fight of the faith and win for yourself the eternal life to which you were called when you made your profession and spoke up for the truth in front of many witnesses."-1 Timothy 6:3-12.

This should serve a guidebook for those in ministry. We have an obligation to teach what has been handed on to us, The Good News, which can never be twisted to fit our own ends. We are told that we must speak up for the truth. We find that truth not in worldly cares or money, but, in Jesus Christ.

In the first few words, St Paul sets everyone straight by saying there is one true faith and that those who do not teach it correctly have something wrong with them. He says they are full of self-conceit. These losers question everything about the Bible, the traditions and the teachings of the Church.

He also stated that men of God, or the churches themselves, that get wrapped up into money are leading themselves into ruin. He does say that "Money is the root of all evils." So why would we want that type of ruin for ourselves? Yes, to live in the world we need money. We should not be obsessed with it as well as envy and unjustly honor those who have a lot of it. They will answer before God for their lives just the same as the rest of us will.

There is no special money club in Heaven. The only true wealth comes from grace, charity, faith, and true Christian love above everything else. Remember that love is contagious and the ultimate solution to every problem. The world improves every time we do something good!

I recently read a passage by the great church father St John Chrysostom who was a bishop and lived in the fourth century. He had a great influence on early Christianity and said the following:

"Do you wish to honor the Body of Christ? Then do not disdain Him when you see Him in rags. After having honored Him in Church with silken vestments, do not leave Him to die of cold outside for lack of clothing. For it is the same Jesus Who says, 'This is My Body' and Who says 'I was hungry but you would not feed Me. Whenever you refused to help one of these least important ones, you refused to help me.' The Body of Christ in the Eucharist demands pure souls, not costly garments. But in the poor He demands all our care. Let us act wisely. Let us honor Christ as He Himself wishes to be honored; the most acceptable honor to one whom we would honor is the honor which He desired, not that which we ourselves imagine. Peter thought he was honoring his Master by not letting the Lord wash his feet; and yet it was just the opposite. Give Him the honor which He Himself has asked for, by giving your money to the poor. Once again what God wants is not so much golden chalices but golden souls."- St. John Chrysostom

In Australia, (not the USA!), an owner of a bus company sold some of his property off and made fifteen million dollars as a result. He then did something that no one expected. He took the money that he had just made and divided it up amongst all his employees equally. Yes! He quietly deposited eight thousand dollars in every employee's bank account. The next day he told them all. Needless to say how astonished they were. The best part of all was that when he was asked why he would do such a thing, he replied, "You take care of your staff and they will take care of you." I am sure that this owner was looking at the big picture for his business. Not only that, but perhaps, he took the Gospel to heart, and look what a difference he made in so many lives.

"Cornelius stared at him in fear. 'What is it, Lord?' he asked. The angel answered, 'Your prayers and gifts to the poor have come up as a memorial offering before God.'" - Acts 10:4

I also have a wonderful account of the story of the Magi...with a twist. It seems that when the Magi went back to Persia and the other parts of the Middle East, there was one wise man who kept the memory of Jesus alive in his heart. He often thought about Jesus and, after thirty years had passed, he decided to go back and look for Him. This was Balthazar. One day he gathered a caravan and stocked it well. It was his intention that when he did meet Jesus, he would present Him with even more lavish gifts in order to honor this great man.

He began his journey and he had gone a mere thirty miles away when he caught sight of a young mother and child out in the cold evening air. They were destitute. Balthazar stopped and took pity upon them and gave them furs with which to wrap themselves and some food. They thanked him and the caravan went on its way. He was several days journey into his trip and he came across a very sick man. He stopped and had a doctor in the group tend to his needs. He then gave the man some gold to help him onto his feet financially. He then continued on.

Two weeks passed and he came upon a group of lepers who were poorly dressed and underfed. He distributed to them the rest of the fine linens and gave them some money and food. He had just about reached Palestine, near the Sea of Galilee, when he encountered a group of homeless children. He took them into town and sold the jewels that he brought to make sure they were fed and clothed. "Now," he said, "I have nothing of value in my caravan." He was saddened, but continued his journey.

The next day, it did not take him long to find out where Jesus was. He sought Him out and was overjoyed at the sight of this most revered soul whom he remembered as just a little baby.

Balthazar fell on his knees before Jesus, he said, "My Lord, how happy I am to have found you. I have thought of You these last thirty years. Please forgive me, Lord, for I am also ashamed." Jesus looked at him with a hint of a question in His face. "Lord," Balthazar said, "Lord, I amassed so many great gifts that I wanted to give you, to honor You."

Jesus then turned to Balthazar and opened His cloak. As Jesus looked at him He smiled and Balthazar's face was astonished as he saw in Jesus' cloak, the faces of all the people he had helped along the way in his journey. Jesus said to him, "Balthazar, Balthazar! Do you see the faces of all these precious ones?" "Yes," he said. Jesus then said, "When you gave what you had to these people who were in need, you gave it to me as well. For I was in every person you encountered, every person you helped." Balthazar then wept. But his tears were not of sorrow, rather they were of joy. He then realized that this was no ordinary man standing in front of him. "Indeed Lord, You are the chosen one of God!" From that moment on, Balthazar followed Jesus from a distance and became close friends with another very good man, Joseph of Arimethia, who welcomed Balthazar as his own brother.

The lesson of the story is clear. We must help our neighbors. We must see Christ in everyone we encounter. The Bible is very clear about this as well when in Matthew's Gospel, it speaks about the last judgment. The good as well as the wicked asked when they aided those in need. The reply was very clear: "What you did for them, you did for Me." To see Christ in others allows us to begin to appreciate the inestimable value of each and every human being. All of creation is good. God holds all of creation within His Sacred Heart and keeps us in being with His constant love. We learn the sacredness of the world around us and our responsibility to govern and preserve it with great responsibility. Remember that we are ultimately responsible for our actions. Jesus did not tell us what kind of house to build, for example; rather, He gave us the foundation with which to build it upon. So many choices are ours to make. Our ability to make choices and decisions is part of what makes us like God. The other part, besides our intellect and will, is our ability to love. Perhaps our love is the part of us that is the most Godlike.

A great theologian in the 13th century spoke of our judgment as not being like a book of recorded acts, both good and bad. Thomas Aquinas stated that when we have our individual judgment, we will go before God and we will see Him as He truly is and He will desire us to be part of Him. If our hearts are full of goodness and love, we will move ourselves to Him and enter into Heaven. If, however, our lives have been characterized by selfishness, we will move away from Him since our souls are not full of charity and true love. Isn't this what sin truly is? Sin is the will knowing something is wrong and deliberately doing it anyway with full freedom to choose. In sinning, we set ourselves up as our own god. It is the ultimate selfishness. When we die, there are no more chances. Our souls are set in what our lives have been. God, in His infinite love, will allow the sinner to have his ultimate final choice: himself. In sin we choose ourselves over all others. What God will do is confirm that choice. This is what Hell truly is. We are alone for eternity. It doesn't matter how many other souls and demons are around us. We have all chosen ourselves as our god. Even the evil angels are finite. They too will suffer from the pain of not doing what was right and their own existence is limited. To illustrate the point, imagine yourself being alone in a dark room for a year. There would be great pain, the pain of emptiness, loneliness, the lack of love; this is the only way to describe it. The fact then is that God, in our particular judgments, will not judge us. We will judge ourselves and then, in the general judgment, God will confirm what we have chosen. It makes sense to me and it also shows the infinite love that God has for each one of us. It also shows the great responsibility we have been given because of our own free will.

St Fulgentius of Ruspe, a very holy man who lived in the fourth century, once said, "My brothers, Christ made love the stairway that would enable all Christians to climb to heaven. Hold fast to it, therefore, in all sincerity, give one another practical proof of it, and by your progress in it, make your ascent together."

We the People

"We the people are the rightful masters of both congress and the courts, not to overthrow the Constitution, but to overthrow the men who would pervert the Constitution."-Abraham Lincoln

Those words, written in the US Constitution, "WE THE PEOPLE," mean that living in a democracy carries with it a great responsibility. We cannot merely sit back and watch the whole thing play out before our eyes like we are doing now. We must participate and our voices be heard.

I took a good hard look at the United States Constitution once again. It still says "WE THE PEOPLE." It does not say, "we big business" or "we the political party" or, "we the decision makers in government." It says "WE THE PEOPLE." Obviously our founders wanted America to be a true democracy, a democracy that reflects the ideas, hopes, desires, and dreams of the American people as a whole. We have the "right to life, liberty and the pursuit of happiness." I interpret these things very literally. First off, there will be no dictatorship over us and no government manipulating us into fear and subservience. It also means that government has the obligation to protect us and our choices for living. It does not mean that we should hurt or step all over each other. Morally, the government has the obligation to protect its citizens. This is interpreted by many developed nations as democratic government, socialized medicine, and programs that develop its citizens through education and other beneficial programs. A capitalist society falls way short of these goals in favor of the rich getting richer and the poor getting poorer (and more subservient). Does this sound familiar?

In late December 2010, the Hungarian government took a bold step and a complete change in direction from its other EU neighbors. Rather than penalize the people for the mistakes of big business, Parliament voted down austerity measures. Instead, it voted for a lowering to a 16% tax on its citizens. It raised taxes on all big business and it imposed heavy levies on banks. It also levied taxes on foreign businesses who took advantage of cheap labor for higher profit. Definitely, this was a step in the right direction. It was a move to balance the economy and protect its citizens from any further financial harm. Also, the Hungarian Parliament made Hungary once again a Christian nation by definition and then moved to outlaw usury in all its forms. Hungary in 2012 definitely benefitted from the move.

We too can change America. We can restore it back to what it should be. The responsibility for that change falls directly on us and our participation in government. We must let our voices be heard and obeyed by those who represent us. Our greatest enemy is apathy and laziness. How many times have we heard it said that "all evil needs to flourish is for good people to sit back and do nothing"? Isn't it so true? Our Pledge of Allegiance says, "one nation under God, with liberty and justice for all." I looked for the references to capitalism and found them absent. Many of the first settlers who came here came in search of religious liberty...to escape religious persecution as the pilgrims did. Our Founding Fathers fought for their liberty. England had oppressed the United States financially and treated them as even less than second class citizens...then the revolution came.

When election results are posted, I am amazed by how many people simply don't vote. They sit back passively and allow others to make their decisions for them. Not a smart idea. The statistics usually show that only 60% of the people vote. Who knows what America would become politically if everyone exercised their right to vote and got involved to stop the changes from happening that hurt us all.

I am also amazed by how many people do not communicate with their elected officials to tell them what's on their minds. We have control of our politicians and we can vote them out when the time comes. Unfortunately, we just let things happen and then wonder how did it ever come to this.

It's true that both candidates for a position are worse and worse still. It's then that we have to demand a change in our system. How about more transparency? How about we demand that the rules change so that no political candidate is bought by the membership of the 1%? We sit back and do nothing. A friend of mine told me that she classifies those who do nothing in the face of these great evils as "sheeple." That is to say they are more like sheep than people. They would rather keep silent and be led to the slaughter than stand up for what is right.

It's our own fault, but it is something that we can change. Change is possible. Even the smallest movement for change will pick up momentum and make a difference. Tell me, if you had a button in front of you that would deliver an electric shock to you, would you press it? I suspect that the answer is NO. So, why do we let ourselves get hurt so easily by the world around us? We have the control. We have the power and the responsibility to better ourselves and the society in which we live. We must build God's Kingdom here on earth. It's true that our ultimate home is in Heaven, but who said we have to make hell here on earth for ourselves?

We must also remember that there is no civilization without conscience. It exists in each of us. It is where the soul touches God. We all share a little piece of it and it reminds us that we are all one family, the human family. So, when one of us suffers, we all suffer. God is real.

I always find the proof of God given by St Anselm to be very intriguing. St Anselm stated that we live in an imperfect universe. We have no experience here on earth of what is truly perfect. Yet, in our minds, we have an ideal of what true perfection should be. St Anselm says that this idea of perfection was infused into us the moment that our souls were created in the womb. At that moment, we touched God. We were also given a conscience at that same moment. Our consciences are part of our free will.

We can form them or malform them in any way we like. God allows this to let us be free.

So too, the concept of freedom is one which we must think about. When, for example, someone claims we are robbing them of their freedom, we should remember that true freedom only implies the choice to do good...or evil. Someone who has murdered someone else has exercised that right. Freedom never provides us with a value system. This is why we have religion. Our faith provides such a guideline to judge and direct. There is no freedom without the Law...God's Law. Our freedom therefore should never imply that everyone lives for himself. Such a thought has led to the dog-eat-dog society and culture where men live and act like wolves in order to prey upon each other ruthlessly to get what they can to have more and more.

Of course, the capitalists do not want true freedom for anyone but themselves. It is not economically feasible to set people free. Actually, it's just the opposite. The best way to make your money is to have people in dependence; just like a drug addiction. It's just like the carrot and stick game. You appeal to people's base passions by appealing to their greed and then snare them in. For example, tell people that they need a TV, they buy one and then become ensnared in paying an ever higher electric bill...or they get the service cut off. Or, they can get even better programming then they have...but they have to pay for it each month. Then they need DVDs, or DVRs, or apps for the phone to record their favorite shows. It never ends.

More and more we are enslaved to owe others money. It's a hard chain to break. Whatever happened to the days when you simply bought a TV set, set up the antenna, and that was it?

Independence in capitalism is a farce. If you're not aggressive and somewhat ruthless, you'll always be a small time player. The only way to become a big player and get ahead is to go play with the big boys and go along with the program. The capitalists have put their own set of ruthless guidelines in place. To try to get ahead as a capitalist and dissent from their methods is financial suicide.

Worse still, we are all forced to survive under capitalist oppression for food, clothing, housing, transportation, and anything else that costs money. As Christians, we need to put a stop to this gouging and immoral raping of the American wallet. We need to be more sufficient upon ourselves and to have a government that puts in regulations that stops the greed mongers from hurting the American people any further.

"But those who desire to be rich fall into temptation, into a snare, into many senseless and hurtful desires that plunge men into ruin and destruction. For the love of money is the root of all evils; it is through this craving that some have wandered away from the faith and pierced their hearts with many pangs." -1 Timothy 6:9-10

I was astonished to see that the tax cuts for the top 1% of the country were allowed to remain in force despite the change in administration. The top 1% have more money than the 99% combined. It would have meant that if the tax cuts were allowed to expire, we would have had an additional $800 billion in the national budget. Didn't anyone else do the math? It is also important to remember that a government budget is like a moral document. It must reflect the interests of equality and the responsible caretaking of all. I am always disheartened to see how many social programs get cut. These programs are most often for the poor and those of no influence in the schemes of power. Those in power are morally responsible for the damages caused by their bad decisions. We become morally responsible if we don't vote them out and put better, more responsible, leadership in power.

"In my many years I have come to the conclusion that one useless man is a shame, two is a law firm, and three or more is a congress." -John Adams.

We must also force our leaders to be responsible. One way is to have the election process revamped so that the 1% are not able to exclude everyone else from the candidacy process. Make the candidacy process affordable for all who wish to run for government.

Continuing on the argument of responsible government, why do we have organizations in government like the EPA or OSHA? The answer is simple. The capitalists, in their greed mongering and lack of responsibility, decided that it was in their best financial interest to simply pollute the earth with the unwanted waste products that they made.

This blatant disregard for everything not profitable has caused millions of innocent people to be harmed and to kill our environment. Lakes and rivers are no longer able to be fished or swam in. We have greenhouse emissions that are poisoning the planet and make it hotter so our weather is changing and the seas are rising. And let's remember that this is the only planet we have. If this one becomes uninhabitable, money really won't matter anymore, will it?

Say what you will, everyone still looked to the President of the US to take control of the situation in the Gulf Coast. Why did he have to? Shouldn't the oil company have done that? They didn't, however; the US stepped in and forced several procedures and extracted money from them to remediate the situation. The multi-million-dollar CEO of the oil company lamented how his life had been turned topsey turvey. He was upset that he could not go yachting with his son in the English Channel the following weekend. He had just destroyed thousands of jobs, millions of gallons of water, and untold land acreage. He ruined the fishing industry. It did not matter to him. He told us in his statements that he did not care. Is this what we want for our country?

We could also talk about the great depression of 2008. Who caused it? How many people have had to suffer, and suffer still, as a result? Is it responsible to put people in office who espouse the rights of big business over the sovereign rights of the American people?

Ronald Reagan once stated: "The scariest words that can ever be uttered are; I am from the government and I am here to help." This man had definitely got it wrong. What did he think should have been said? "I am from big business and I am here to help?" That would be a joke. Certainly those words would only be said to avoid an image problem with the corporation in question and, thus, protect profits in the long run. It is the responsibility of government to protect its people. Business will only protect its profits.

Well, let's face it. Business is there to make money. Businesses are not there for the welfare and well-being of the people. That is what government is for. To make government smaller so that capitalism can run rampant is not the ideal of democracy. That is far from it. It will lead us into a form of dictatorship where the dollar reigns supreme. Isn't that what is happening right now? Isn't that the definition of a plutonomy?

Reagan also said that the government was there to protect the people and not run their lives. Well, where is government now to protect us from the financial terrorists? Are our lives our own? The size of government is not the issue. Whether the government is dysfunctional or not is the greater issue. If government ran the way it was supposed to, we wouldn't have the problems that we do today.

I think the downfall of America is also in the brainwashing we have now. If the government has to give out "handouts," then those needy people are losers. Get rid of welfare and Medicare, they say. They want us to privatize everything. How many people out there are disabled, for example, and cannot work? Are they losers? What the government is doing now is really sugarcoating all the handouts that they give to the rich. In other words, handouts to the poor are bad and handouts to the rich are good? Really? The tax breaks and the laws that cater to the rich and corporations simultaneously rape the middle class and the poor. Maybe the government should be more transparent about this and start their chant, "Alms for the rich! Alms for the rich!"

Why were there anti-trust laws put into place? These laws prevented monopolies from rising that would immediately cause the American people to pay more for much needed goods and services. Big business has as its agenda to grow and grow and even control government itself to further their ends for global financial domination. Remember, a small government is easier to control.

It seems to me that the capitalists love to gripe about ideologies such as socialism, communism and dictatorships. The sad fact is that the very capitalists will bring us to a dictatorship one day. Think it's farfetched? Well, think about how much big business already controls our lives and our governments. How many times have we heard that a strong government can be judged by its economy? Whatever happened to a strong government being judged by the health, happiness and well-being of its people? Or being judged by its morals?

I often amuse myself with the thought of how the US government is the best government that money can buy!

Capitalists have tried to make a very slithery argument that tries to twist democracy together with capitalism. The capitalists state that this is what the people want. What nation of people wants to be spit on by the wealthy elite while they live in squalor? Democracy must never be used to justify any course of action. First and foremost, democracy must have within it the safeguards necessary to protect its citizens from both financial and physical harm. It's like freedom of speech. One must be free to voice one's opinion. However, if that opinion would lead to any form of harm to others, especially those who follow true morality, then it is no longer freedom of speech but rather a platform to incite harm and counterproductive to democracy.

Certainly, Christ did not tell us to retreat from the world. He wanted us to live in the world but to be children of the light. I think that true scientific advancement, for example, is in line with Gospel values. The earth, and indeed the universe, are ours to discover and to master (with responsibility and Christian ethics). I look forward to the day when men walk on the surface of Mars or get out to the moons of Saturn.

We cannot deny that God's creation includes physical, material things. His plan for mankind includes labor, which produces both physical goods and intangible services. It is clear from scripture that He intends for individuals to have the right to own these things as their own personal property. This is supported by two of the Ten Commandments, namely, "You shall not steal" and "You shall not covet." These two commandments affirm that something belongs to one person and not to someone else. It is not an invitation, however, to be selfish. It is an opportunity to express the love of God in practicing genuine virtue through giving. We help others through our own generosity and philanthropy. Ultimately, let us always remember that God is the owner of all things.

"For every beast of the forest is mine, the cattle on a thousand hills. I know every bird of the mountains, and everything that moves in the field is Mine. If I were hungry, I would not tell you; for the world is Mine, and all it contains." -Psalms 50:10

The Poor

"If anyone has material possessions and sees his brother in need but has no pity on him, how can the love of God be in him? Dear children, let us not love with words or tongue but with actions and in truth." -1 John 3:17-18

One day, the father of an extremely well to do family decided to take a ride in the countryside with his children in their Bentley. As his children got into the car, he laughed and told them that they were going on a field trip, like the school outings they take to Europe when school is out of session. The father told them that this time around they were going to see how the poor people live. Those people who are even lower than the hired help.

The father had found a poor farm which had a very large old house on it. Probably dated to a time when the farmer and his wife had several children. It was definitely run down, but it was clean. The children spent a few days there and actually helped the farmer and his wife with the chores which the children found quite fascinating.

When the father came to pick the children up, he asked them how their little field trip went. "What did you learn from this experience?" the father asked.

The first son said, "It was great, Dad." The other children agreed with him. "Why?" the father asked them. They all sounded off one after the other: "Well, we have one small dog that needs to be pampered; they had four dogs that helped and protected them." Another child said, "We have a pool that is large, but they have a river and creek that seemed endless with frogs and fish to watch and explore." Still one of the other children added, "And we have those stupid little lawn lanterns in the backyard, they have the stars at night and the moon to light the way." The oldest boy, eager to add more information stated, "Well, they have such huge wonderful fields with fresh air and wonderful food that they grow themselves. We have the smog of the city; we go to that stupid food store to buy our own food." The girl then interjected, "We have servants who serve us, and they have their own community in which they constantly help each other out." The littlest one wanted to say something as well. She told her father that, "we have a big fence and a gate around our property to keep us safe and protect us and we don't talk to people, they have their friends to help them and keep them safe."

At this point the father did not know what to say to them. He wasn't sure if the trip actually had the effect that he wanted it to have. It was at that point that the oldest son said to his father, "thanks Dad for showing us how poor we are." The other children agreed.

This is a great responsibility that God puts into our hands, namely that we are the custodians of the world and all it contains. We, therefore, are also responsible to spread part of what we have to take care of the poor. Charity, in all forms, is proscribed by the Bible. Jesus Himself said that we would always have the poor with us. We show ourselves as the lights of grace and love. Will it not be Christ Himself on the great Day of Judgment that will say, "Whatsoever you do to the least of my brethren, that you do unto Me"?

I think at this point, we need to define "the poor." To be poor in this world does not only mean abject poverty. It means those who have suffered or continue to suffer great hardship. For example, how about the elderly couple whose husband had a job at Enron? The man worked hard and saved responsibly for their retirement. Along come the executives that dealt with greed and irresponsibility with the retirement plans of thousands of workers. We should call it financial terrorism at its best. Now the couple has no retirement savings. They are the poor.

What about the individual who works hard but is kept down by the greed of the "big boss"? Many in management, especially upper management, make lots of money while those in the actual workforce are worked to the bone and lucky to have minimum wage? They are the poor.

The poor, often, are educated as well. They have been dealt hard knocks in the job market. How many college grads get out there and find nothing and end up living at home with a huge debt hanging over their heads? They are the poor as well.

What about those who have been so heinously blacklisted for whistle blowing or for standing up for human rights?

The employers don't care whom they hurt. So these heroic people are left out in the cold to suffer for doing what is right. Many of them have become the poor.

What about those who are born with a mental deficiency or are challenged physically? The permissive will of God has allowed them to have a great many disadvantages in their lives here on earth. They are the poor.

How about those who are getting taxed out of existence while the rich enjoy their tax loopholes and pay nothing or next to nothing? They are the poor as well.

What about the man who works hard all his life and gets sick? It could be due to the fault of the business world, such as the asbestos problem and mesothelioma. It could be cancer due to the deception of the tobacco industry. Or, it could be genetics as well. Most often, and sometimes with great difficulty on the part of the individual, these people are relegated to the disability pool. Guess what, they are the poor as well.

These are just some examples. Our society today tries to make us think of the poor in the lowest terms in our culture. Perhaps we should make a distinction between low class and the poor. One can be low class in any socioeconomic level. Hey, look at how many rich people are low class! They have no manners. They scream and cry like spoiled babies until they get their way and have no consideration of others! They deceive and steal. How many times have we seen this behavior? It seems that we are also taught to make excuses for them, why? Just because they are rich does not entitle them to be jerks.

So let me ask you, reader, if you lost your job right now, how long before you became poor? How long before your resources ran dry? The average job search takes many, many months. How many people have taken more than a year to find a new job?

It seems to me that the poor have so many wonderful things to offer the world. Many show great hospitality. They are closer to God and they show charity. Many have a wisdom that is particular to them and their situation in the world. They have a wonderful point of view that is unclouded by excessive wealth or greed. They are often truly more spiritual as well. They also seem to have more common sense and have to live by it every day.

One day I heard a very simple man say that, "He never let his schooling interfere with his education." This is a truly wise thought for practical living.

Perhaps now we should rethink our ideas about the poor. So many people today are poor through no fault of their own.

I remember one day walking through a very wealthy neighborhood just north of New York City. I was with a Franciscan friar. As we walked on the side of the rural country street, a woman in a six figure luxury car came speeding past us and almost knocked us over. She even gave us a dirty look before almost mowing us down. I remembered the words of that Franciscan very clearly after the incident. He told me that he had truly found the most abject poverty there, where he lived. He told me how the people where poor in manners and in charity. They deprived themselves of the love of God. He told me how selfish they were. "Their money," he said, "had blinded them to love." They had no love within them. Their wealth had corrupted them and infected them with the worst kind of poverty: the spiritual kind. Their quest for real happiness was here on the earth. How ridiculous to grasp at a passing, fleeting moment of pleasure while ignoring the consequences of what is to come. This type of poverty is one we need to fight as well.

It was the great St Augustine of Hippo who wrote, "A man's poverty before God is judged by the disposition of his heart and not by his coffers."

In the Old Testament, the prophet Isaiah is quick to reprove the people as to how they should treat others. It echoes in the words of Jesus 1000 years later.

"Is not this the kind of fasting I have chosen: to lose the chains of injustice and untie the cords of the yoke, to set the oppressed free and break every yoke? Is it not to share your food with the hungry and to provide the poor wanderer with shelter—when you see the naked, to clothe him, and not to turn away from your own flesh and blood?"-Isaiah 58:6-7

Physical and spiritual poverty is truly a weapon of mass destruction! Ignoring poverty can wreak havoc on all of us. It leads to many negatives that break the harmony of our culture, like an increase in crime. Those in poverty are more likely to cause social unrest in various forms as well.

Look what happened in South America in the 1900s when big business suppressed various countries to the point of social revolt; and revolt they did. Better still look at France in the late 1700s when the poor had had enough. There was a total revolution and the king himself lost his head. The power of the people, especially as an angry mob, is more formidable than any national army. Look how they totally changed the nation around!

The capitalists try every way they can to stop the poor from voting. They try by making it harder for them to be heard in the voting booth and to limit their choices. The poor then become apathetic. That apathy allows those who do vote a stronger voice. It then becomes easier for those who wish to gain power and push their agendas to get in and change government around. If there had been an opportunity for the poor to have a say, perhaps the French revolution and its aftermath would not have occurred.

Nowadays, there are moves by state governments to limit the voting rights of its people through required voter registration. This specifically targets the elderly, minorities, and the disabled in creating additional obstacles for them to vote. It especially hurts the poor by robbing them of their democratic voice.

Compassion and caring for the poor are among the Bible's greatest concerns. When God called the Israelites to live in a community under His covenant, he established several laws whose purpose was to provide for the needs of the poor.

The tithe in the third year of every seven-year cycle was to go to the poor.

"At the end of every third year you shall bring out all the tithe of your produce in that year, and shall deposit it in your town [...] the alien, the orphan and the widow who are in your town, shall come and eat and be satisfied, in order that the Lord your God may bless you in all the work of your hand which you do."- Deuteronomy 14:28-29

Some of each person's agricultural harvest was to be left for the poor.

"Now when you reap the harvest of your land, you shall not reap to the very corners of your field, neither shall you gather the gleanings of your harvest. Nor shall you glean your vineyard, nor shall you gather the fallen fruit of your vineyard; you shall leave them for the needy and the stranger. I am the Lord your God." -Leviticus 19:9-10

The poor had the right to interest-free loans and food priced at cost value.

"Now in case a countryman of yours becomes poor and his means with regard to you falter, then you are to sustain him, like a stranger or a sojourner that he may live with you. Do not take usurious interest from him, but revere your God, that your countryman may live with you. You shall not give him your silver at interest, nor your food for gain." -Leviticus 25:35-37

The Old Testament takes great lengths to discuss powerful people who oppress the poor, and rulers who failed to come to their defense and give them justice. It has much to say about the general rights of every human being. For example:

"Woe to those who are heroes in drinking wine, and valiant men in mixing strong drink; who justify the wicked for a bribe and take away the rights of the ones who are in the right."-Isaiah 5:22-23

The above Biblical passage is regarding bribery and corruption. We see politicians granting special favors, concessions rulings, etc., to those who would pay them the most money.

"Do you become a king because you are competing in cedar? Did not your father eat and drink and do justice and righteousness? Then it was well with him. He pled the cause of the needy: Then it was well. Is not that what it means to know Me? Declares the Lord. But your eyes and your heart are intent only upon dishonest gain, and on shedding innocent blood, and on practicing oppression and extortion." -Jeremiah 22:15-17

Jeremiah's point here deals with the seizing the property of others by violence. Having failed to obtain fields and houses through legitimate means, these men took the property of others by force. The best Biblical example of this is King Ahab, who was angry with his neighbor, Naboth, and had his neighbor put to death so he could take possession of his vineyard, which he had refused to sell him (see 1 Kings 21).

"Hear this, you who trample on the needy, to do away with the humble of the land, saying, 'When will the new moon be over, so that we may buy grain, and the Sabbath, that we may open the wheat market, to make the bushel smaller and the shekel bigger, and to cheat with dishonest scales, so as to buy the helpless for money, and the needy for a pair of sandals, and that we may sell the refuse of the wheat?'"- Amos 8:4-6.

The prophet Amos deals here with the subject of not defending the rights of the consumer. As we have already seen, the poor had certain legal rights to the resources of others in the Old Testament law (interest-free loans, food sold at cost, etc.). Then, as now, people still seek to deny the poor these rights.

"Woe to those who scheme out iniquity who work our evil on their beds! When morning comes, they do it, for it is in the power of their hands. They covet fields and then seize them, and houses, and take them away. They rob a man of his house, a man and his inheritance." -Micah 2:2

Here the prophet Micah sounds as though he was dealing with our own housing crisis today. Could he be describing a vision that he had also for the distant future dealing with predatory lending practices and derivatives?

In Nehemiah 5, certain members of the Hebrew community had to borrow money to pay the king's tax. The lenders, however, charged them interest. This was strictly forbidden. Nehemiah did defend them in this case. In this sense, the redistribution of resources can also be argued and be considered part of Old Testament justice.

In the early life of the church, it does not appear that there were any attempts to help the entire population of the poor in the Roman Empire. It seems that the Church directed her care only towards her own. Interestingly enough, the Roman government itself had its own social welfare system in place for the poor. It was St Paul who spoke about the Roman government; we note that he never said anything against its policies regarding the less fortunate.

It is also important to point out that the mere fact of economic inequality is not in and of itself in violation of Biblical principles. We see that the Bible does realize that sometimes poverty and financial misfortune are the result of bad choices by the individual. For example, it can be the result of laziness or lack of proper direction:

"I passed by the field of the sluggard and by the vineyard of the man lacking sense; and behold, it was completely overgrown with thistles, its surface was covered with nettles, and its stone wall was broken down."- Proverbs 24:30-31

On the other hand, the Bible does acknowledge that some people do prosper because of their determination and hard work. It sees no immorality in honest acquisition.

"Poor is he who works with a negligent hand, but the hand of the diligent makes rich." -Proverbs 10:4

So what then becomes the proper Biblical approach to wealth? Ultimately it will be that those who are not attached to their wealth and live a moral life will attain the Kingdom of God.

In the New Testament, the focus shifts more to equality for all. The best example would be how the early Christians lived; commune-like in their structures. In this system, it is clear that God wants each person to have the necessary resources to provide for themselves and their families.

"All the believers were one in heart and mind. No one claimed that any of his possessions was his own, but they shared everything they had. With great power the apostles continued to testify to the resurrection of the Lord Jesus, and much grace was upon them all. There was no needy among them. For from time to time, those who owned lands or houses sold them, and put it at the apostles' feet, and it was distributed to anyone as he had need." -Acts 4:32-35

It must be noted that providing to the poor is never intended as a means for the unscrupulous to have a way to take advantage of the system. In fact, those who are lazy or unwilling to work are even shunned from the community.

"For even when we were with you, we gave you this rule. 'If a man will not work, he shall not eat.' We hear that some among you are idle. They are not busybodies. Such people we command and urge in the Lord Jesus Christ to settle down and earn the bread they eat [...]If anyone does not obey our instruction in this letter, take special note of him. Do not associate with him, in order that he may feel ashamed." -2 Thessalonians 3:10-12, 14

There are two additional things that should be noted about the aid given to the poor through the church.

First, the family of the poor person, not the community, has the primary responsibility for his or her aid. Writing to Timothy, Paul wrote:

"If any woman who is a believer has widows in her family, she should help them and not let the church be burdened with them, so that the church can help those widows who are really in need." -1 Timothy 5:16

The second and more interesting point to note is that the aim of the care for the poor is to provide for their basic material needs only. The Bible teaches that while our material prosperity may vary over time, we are not entitled to have more than our basic needs met at any given point in time:

"For we brought nothing into the world, and we can take nothing out of it. But if we have food and clothing, we will be content with that." -1 Timothy 6:7-8

Likewise, the New Testament church also adopted the same principles, if not the same exact practices:

"What good is it, my brothers, if a man claims to have faith but has no deeds? Can such faith save him? Suppose a brother or sister is without clothes and daily food. If one of you says to him, 'Go, I wish you well; keep warm and well fed,' but does nothing about his physical needs, what good is it?" -James 2:14-16

Likewise, in the Olivet Discourse, Jesus says that those who did not feed, clothe, and water the least of His brethren will not go into eternal life (Matthew 25:31-46).

I do wish to make one point clear that may need some clarification: When we help the poor, the Christian intention is not to produce equality but rather to help them to produce this effect on their own. This is the great difference between Christian social goals and the immoral atheistic socialism; the latter of which I do not endorse.

"He who gives to the poor will lack nothing, but he who closes his eyes to them receives many curses."-Proverbs 28:27

In order to put such ideals into practice, we need to start small. We can start in our very own parishes and church communities. If enough churches start these practices, it will start a general movement...in the right direction. We are the people of God and the choices are ultimately ours to make.

One example of putting Gospel values in motion started last year when a national concession decided in one of its Michigan restaurants to ask its customers for a donation for the food they received. The suggested donation was the actual price charged for the food. Studies showed that 40% of customers paid a fair amount in line with the suggested donation. 20% of all customers actually gave more than the suggested donation. 20% gave less than the suggested donation. The final 20% was unaccounted for. It would seem that those who were unable to give fell into this category. The critics of this program said it would never work. The restaurant chain recently announced that they have been making a profit. In fact, they chose another store in the Northeast to follow this same method of business. Many fellow business owners have criticized this vehemently. What is their motivation to not do the same? How many of these business owners who are against this are Christians themselves?

"He who is kind to the poor lends to the LORD, and He will reward him for what he has done." -Proverbs 19:17

Finally, a program called "D diving" came into being. The name of the program is somewhat misleading. It's not about something degrading in which a person forages through any old dumpster to see what he can eat. Such a practice could be extremely hazardous to one's health! The program is about going around to various grocery stores and asking them for the products that they would normally throw out just as they pass their freshness expiration date. Grocery stores throw away tons of good food every year. This excessive waste can be put to good use. Again, we are not talking about green meat or moldy bread or cheese. We are talking about day-old bread or meat that has just reached freshness expiration. These safe products do not need to be thrown away. One man, in implementing this program, wrote to all the CEOs of different grocery chains. It was no surprise to him that he received no response. He then went around to the store managers of different neighborhood grocery stores and made agreements with many of them to get the food before it landed in the actual dumpster. So volunteers for various organizations go around and collect these products before they are chucked. Many grocery stores have joined in this effort to feed the hungry in this way. Throwing good food away is clearly a sin!

"When you are harvesting in your field and you overlook a sheaf, do not go back to get it. Leave it for the alien, the fatherless and the widow, so that the LORD your God may bless you in all the work of your hands. When you beat the olives from your trees, do not go over the branches a second time. Leave what remains for the alien, the fatherless and the widow. When you harvest the grapes in your vineyard, do not go over the vines again. Leave what remains for the alien, the fatherless and the widow." - Deuteronomy 24:19-21

Capitalism and Christianity

"Passover was at hand, and Jesus went up to Jerusalem. And found in the Temple those that sold oxen and sheep and doves, and the changers of money sitting: And when He had made a small scourge of cords, He drove them all out of the Temple, and the sheep, and the oxen; and poured out the changers' money, and overthrew the tables." -John 2:13-15

Isn't it amazing that the only time in His visible life here upon earth, Jesus gets violent against the money changers? He whips them, throws their coins about and overturns their tables. The money changers can be equated with the early banking profession. They did their business there in the Temple and with the blessing of the Jewish high priests. The bankers didn't set up shop for free. I am sure that the priests received some recompense for allowing them to operate in the Temple precincts. We can therefore conclude that Jesus' only act of violence ever was against the bankers and the financial industry! He told them that they had turned His Father's House into a den of thieves. He did call them thieves!

Jesus had just made His triumphant entry into Jerusalem. The peoples' respect for Jesus was at its peak. This move against the financial industry in Jerusalem was not seen by the bankers in a positive light. It is quite possible that behind the scenes, they were the catalyst that helped to get Jesus crucified. Enough evidence can be intimated here to support this idea.

In fact, in St Mark's Gospel after this account in 11:18 it states, "Which when the chief priests and the Scribes had heard, they sought how they might destroy Him. For they feared Him, because the whole multitude was in admiration of His doctrine."

What does this tell us? First off, Jesus called the money changers a "den of thieves." This description of them is recorded in three of the Gospel accounts. The fourth, St John's Gospel, has Him speaking to the dove sellers not to "traffic" goods in the Temple precincts. For St Mark's Gospel to say that the people were in admiration of His doctrine was an admission by the evangelist that the financial industry, even back then, was morally corrupt and extremely evil. Obviously the Jewish clergy at the time were in full agreement with the bankers. Let's face it, the bankers paid for their stalls and kept a steady income coming in to the Temple coffers. The financial industry, even in ancient times, has always been a corrupt "den of thieves." Christ Himself called them this term. What does that tell us?

It's not hard to see that capitalism and Christianity are completely opposed to one another. Capitalism is the worship of money and its acquisition to fulfill the need of having. Its aim is total self-gratification. Its end is selfishness and greed.

Again, all forms of capitalism are "founded on the selfish individual." Capitalism consciously appeals to the individual's inclination to acquire goods, to accumulate wealth. Whether in order to be better protected, to have the wherewithal to lead a comfortable life in the future, or to count for something in society. The inclination can become an addiction, the accumulation of wealth an end in itself. This is what Christian ethics defined as covetousness, cupidity, or avarice.

The other driving force behind capitalist economics, apart from the individual's striving for personal gain, is competition. Our fellow human beings are either our helpers or our competitors. As family members, employees or customers, they can help us; as competitors, they can harm us. Workers and employees, even when treated well, are still a "cost factor." And, if they set up in business on their own, they become our competitors.

In the New Testament, our fellow man is not our competitor but our "neighbor." The ethical code of the New Testament revolves entirely around this relationship with our "neighbor." Not because man is intrinsically a social animal, but because he is dependent on his fellow men and cannot live without them. These are the relationships that shape our lives. "Thou shalt love thy neighbor as thyself." Asked the question "Who is my neighbor?", Jesus replies by telling the parable of the Good Samaritan. The Samaritans were not Jews, but despised foreigners. So our neighbor is not necessarily our biological brother or someone of like mind, but the individual who is most in need of our help and care.

"Sell your possessions and give to the poor. Provide purses for yourselves that will not wear out, a treasure in heaven that will not be exhausted, where no thief comes near and no moth destroys." -Luke 12:33

It's amazing to me how many churches out there have softened the message of Jesus or twisted it to a point where it is no longer recognizable. How many pastors and priests are teaching about how to achieve one's own financial success? "Remember that we cannot punish the successful!" they tell us. How more un-Christian can you get?

"Prayer is good when accompanied by fasting, almsgiving, and righteousness. A little with righteousness is better than much with wrongdoing. It is better to give alms than to treasure up gold. For almsgiving delivers from death, and it will purge away every sin. Those who perform deeds of charity and of righteousness will have fullness of life." -Tobit 12:8-9

I also have an issue with one of the largest Christian denominations. Recently they have aligned themselves with one of the political groups. Why they have done this, I cannot say. This particular political group is all about the 1%. Together, they claim to fight against abortion. I have nothing against fighting abortion. I myself am pro-life, as every Christian should be. My issue is with the fact that they focus upon this one point and no other. They make the political landscape a joke by making the moral choice to be a "one issue voter." This wears their credibility thin when they try to preach the Gospel. There are so many other issues to contend with as well. What about charity? What about caring for others like the homeless and the hungry? Aren't these pro-life issues as well?

The question has also been raised as to an accurate definition of "Pro-Life" vs. "Pro-Birth." The answer lies within the distinctions between the two terms and in what they cover. Someone who is "Pro-Birth" is most definitely against abortion, however, does that individual qualify as "Pro-Life"?

In the Gospel narratives, we have a clear understanding from Christ of what it means to be "Pro-life." For one to be "Pro-Life," one must actively participate to protect and defend all stages of the earthly existence of the human person. For example, Jesus tells us to help the poor. He instructs us that we must feed the hungry, clothe the naked, help the oppressed. We must also love one another as God loves us. I have encountered groups, and even churches, that seem to have totally missed the mark on this.

I find it to be absolute insanity to have someone fight for the rights of the unborn and then stop right there. The dignity of the human person does not cease after childbirth. In fact, the human person has its greatest challenges outside the womb. Therefore, we as Christians, to profess to be "Pro-Life," must consume ourselves in love and compassion for all people. We must care for each other at every stage of life. It is a supreme irony to be antiabortion and then leave the person alone, defenseless, oppressed, and demonized.

Our society today demonizes the poor. It glorifies the rich. Our society wants to worship money above all other things and, in doing so, debase and demoralize the human person. Our society places our intrinsic worth upon the altar of hedonism with no remorse. It has been shown that when the poor, for example, have access to their God given rights of housing, health care, education, and social services, they are less likely to think about having an abortion. The poor are the social group with the highest percentage of abortions. Doesn't it make sense to provide for them as we have been told to do by Christ?

In St Matthew's Gospel, we read the following passage:

"When the Son of Man comes in his glory, and all the angels with him, then he will sit on the throne of his glory. All the nations will be gathered before him, and he will separate people one from another as a shepherd separates the sheep from the goats, and he will put the sheep at his right hand and the goats at the left. Then the king will say to those at his right hand, 'Come, you that are blessed by my Father, inherit the kingdom prepared for you from the foundation of the world; for I was hungry and you gave me food, I was thirsty and you gave me something to drink, I was a stranger and you welcomed me, I was naked and you gave me clothing, I was sick and you took care of me, I was in prison and you visited me.' Then the righteous will answer him, 'Lord, when was it that we saw you hungry and gave you food, or thirsty and gave you something to drink? And when was it that we saw you a stranger and welcomed you, or naked and gave you clothing? And when was it that we saw you sick or in prison and visited you?' And the king will answer them, 'Truly I tell you, just as you did it to one of the least of these who are members of my family, you did it to me.' Then he will say to those at his left hand, 'You that are accursed, depart from me into the eternal fire prepared for the devil and his angels; for I was hungry and you gave me no food, I was thirsty and you gave me nothing to drink, I was a stranger and you did not welcome me, naked and you did not give me clothing, sick and in prison and you did not visit me.' Then they also will answer, 'Lord, when was it that we saw you hungry or thirsty or a stranger or naked or sick or in prison, and did not take care of you?' Then he will answer them, 'Truly I tell you, just as you did not do it to one of the least of these, you did not do it to me.' And these will go away into eternal punishment, but the righteous into eternal life."- Matthew 25:31-46

Jesus is extremely clear and concise on how we are to treat one another. He tells us to see His presence inside of everyone we encounter. He is also quite clear that those who would seek their own pleasures and selfishness, which is a detriment to others, would be sent away into eternal punishment.

My heart sank in sadness as I listened to the warped and twisted words of one radio announcer recently as he proclaimed, "Oh! We can't punish the successful!" His message being that we should not touch those who have reached financial success regardless of how they did it. It is the old rouse of letting the rich get richer at the expense of the rest of us. That message is definitely not Christian!

We must care for one another. This life on earth is a test for us. We will either pass or fail and there are no "do-overs." We are only "Pro-Life" when we love each other and do what is right and good in the eyes of Almighty God. If we err by seeing this concept as protecting the unborn only, then we have failed fundamentally in our understanding of the Gospel's message. ALL LIFE IS SACRED FROM CONCEPTION TO EARTHLY FINISH. We, as Christians, have an obligation to uphold this value.

In his Letter to the Galatians, Paul summarizes the ethics of Christian charity thus: "Bear one another's burdens, and so fulfill the law of Christ" (Galatians 6:2).This contrast with the capitalist credo could not be more starkly formulated. To the capitalist, this must appear nonsensical. How can an economy even function, let alone grow, if everyone is intent on bearing the burdens of others? Surely it is much more productive and cost-effective if everyone looks out for themselves? But this is not the case. Greed makes things worse, not better.

"Now this was the sin of your sister Sodom: She and her daughters were arrogant, overfed and unconcerned; they did not help the poor and needy."- Ezekiel 16:49

I find it interesting that the prophet Ezekiel did not refer to the sin of Sodom as something sexual; rather, it was something societal. Was the real sin of Sodom... a form of capitalism?

Again, in capitalism everything has its price. And that price is determined by the law of supply and demand. Not so in the New Testament. Jesus tells the story of a "householder" and owner of a vineyard, who goes out early in the morning to hire laborers to work in his vineyard. He promises them payment of one denarius for the day's work – the sum that a family needs to live on. Throughout the day, until the early evening, the householder continues to hire more laborers who are standing around waiting for work. He says he will give them "whatsoever is right."

At the end of the day, he pays them all one denarius, regardless of whether they have worked for twelve hours or one hour. This annoys the early birds in particular. The householder asks: "Why be jealous because I am kind?" (Matthew 20:15). Each receives what he and his family need. To give any less would be mean. But this runs counter, not only to the rules of capitalism, but also to the workers' own sense of justice. I will expound upon this parable in greater detail in a later chapter.

Christianity is the worship of Christ. It has as its aim the worship of God and to be filled with His love. Its ultimate goal is our salvation through oneness in heaven with God; the true source of all love. This love is also spread to others for the benefit of all. Remember the First Commandment? Or how about when Jesus said that you cannot serve two masters..."you cannot serve both God and Mammon" (Matthew 6:24). It is true that we need to use money in our society in order to succeed with our lives. But is it true that he who has the most toys when he dies wins? When one is born into the world, one has only one's self and one's nakedness. When one dies, one will only have one's self with one's choices, experiences, actions, and one's love of either one's self or God. What fool thinks that he will be able to bribe God to get into Heaven. Remember the story of Lazarus the beggar?

"There was a rich man, who was clothed in purple and fine linen and who feasted sumptuously every day. And at his gate lay a poor man named Lazarus, full of sores, who desired to be fed with what fell from the rich man's table; moreover the dogs came and licked his sores. The poor man died and was carried by the angels to Abraham's bosom. The rich man also died and was buried; and in Hades, being in torment, he lifted up his eyes, and saw Abraham far off and Lazarus in his bosom. And he called out, `Father Abraham, have mercy upon me, and send Lazarus to dip the end of his finger in water and cool my tongue; for I am in anguish in this flame.' But Abraham said, `Son, remember that you in your lifetime received your good things, and Lazarus in like manner evil things; but now he is comforted here, and you are in anguish.'" - Luke 16:19-25

It would seem that riches to any great extent are as a hindrance to us and a distraction from what really matters here on earth.

"Riches prick us with a thousand troubles in getting them, as many cares in preserving them, and yet more anxiety in spending them, and with grief in losing them."-St. Francis of Assisi

If we devote our lives to the acquisition of wealth, how can we truly better ourselves and those around us?

Isn't it amazing how Brazil has actually survived unscathed by the financial meltdown that began in 2008? Consider the fact that they never went on board with the World Trade Organization. Brazil did not see the attraction of going global. Perhaps her president realized the long term effects and negative repercussions associated with the WTO and the IMF. Certainly, she was not a victim of greed. As a result, Brazil is in a much better shape than any other country near her; in fact, even in the world. The other exceptions are Russia, China and India. They also are not part of the IMF.

Capitalistic propaganda has hurt us. Listen to the words that they use to snare everyone into their trap: They promise wealth to everyone who works hard and invests. Tell me, how many rich people do you know? Really rich?

Not many I bet. The capitalist will tempt you using your own greed and instill in you a false hope that someday, you too will be rich. We are slowly becoming slaves to the wealthy. Even in our universities, there are classes taught to form young minds into the capitalist mindset and create a character more receptive to economic slavery. Recently I heard a young man on the radio state how this is a great time to be a capitalist. I asked myself how. Foreclosures are staggering, the job market is horrible, and commodities like gas are through the roof. People are struggling. Just how is this a great time? Unless, of course, you're on the receiving end of the financial balance? I dare say not too many. Just remember that the only effect of working hard may be that the rich get richer and that you will be very physically tired!

It's also a well-known fact that the WTO has as part of its agenda, to strip all workers worldwide of the rights and protections that they have. They seek a one world government with a privileged few controlling everything.

In December 2010, the US Congress debated and passed the "tax cuts." These "cuts" allow the top upper class, the 1%, those who make seven figures a year, to have ridiculously huge tax breaks while the other classes, especially the poorer ones, to suffer greatly by paying a disproportionately higher amount of taxes. A certain political group insists upon maintaining this tax break for the rich. I ask you, where is the justice in this? Worse still, why aren't Americans outraged by this and calling their representatives to stop this injustice? Those in favor of retaining this injustice seek to frighten people by telling them that if the cuts are dropped, there will be even less jobs out there for people. We are told that the tax cuts actually help to stimulate job growth. What a joke this is! This is a scare tactic, once again, to push the agenda of making the wealthy even wealthier. Again, I ask, where we are seeing more job creation as a result of these ridiculous tax cuts?

It's just so funny to see just how many wealthy people say that they are Christian. These are the very ones who defend their enormous wealth. Wasn't it Jesus in the Sermon on the Mount who stated: "Blessed are the poor, for yours is the Kingdom of God" (Luke 6:20)? Or how about in Mark's Gospel when He said, "Blessed are the poor in spirit, for theirs is the Kingdom of Heaven" (Mark 5:30)? How can one justify capitalism with these words?

We need to go back to the Bible to look at just what the Christian view of economics should be. For example, the law that goes against charging interest comes from the passage in Exodus in the Old Testament. It states, "If you lend money to one of your poor neighbors, among my people, you shall not act like an extortioner toward him by demanding interest from him." The Old Testament repeats this statement twenty-two times. Psalm 15:1-5 says, "Yahweh, who can find a home in your tent, who can dwell on your holy mountain? Whoever lives blamelessly, who acts uprightly, who speaks the truth from the heart [...]

who asks no interest on loans, who takes no bribe to harm the innocent. No one who so acts can ever be shaken."

Deuteronomy 15:1-11 orders the cancellation of all debts at the end of every seventh year. And it cautions against refusing to lend to one in need because this time is near. So your loan will never be repaid to you. So what? The Lord will take care of you. But if you refuse one in need, the Lord will hold you "guilty of sin [...] I command you to open your hand to your countrymen who are poor and needy."

The New Testament is not silent on the issue of finances either. Most of the statements made are against those who have great wealth.

"Next, a word to you who are rich. Weep and wail over the miserable fate overtaking you: your riches [...] will be evidence against you and consume your flesh like fire [...] You have lived on the land in wanton luxury, gorging yourselves — and on the day appointed for your slaughter."- James 5:1.

Let's look at the words of Christ when He said:

"If you wish to be perfect, go, sell what you have and give to the poor, and you will have treasure in heaven. Then come, follow me. [...] Amen, I say to you, it will be hard for one who is rich to enter the kingdom of heaven. Again I say to you, it is easier for a camel to pass through the eye of a needle than for one who is rich to enter the kingdom of God."-Matthew 19:21-24

It's no surprise that the first Christians were very serious in how they applied the teachings of Christ into their daily lives and, of course, into their economic dealings with others. The Didache taught in its writings, "Do not claim that anything is your own." About a 100 years after the death of Christ, we have Clement of Alexandria who said, "All possessions are by nature unrighteous; when one possesses them for personal advantage and does not bring them into the common stock for those in need." The great and learned church Father, Basil the Great, around the year 400 A.D. said, "That bread which you keep belongs to the hungry; that coat in your closet, to the naked."

The great Doctor of the Church, St. Augustine said, "Business is in itself an evil." It is interesting to note that St Jerome, the great Biblical scholar responsible for recopying the Bible for the advantage of all who normally disagreed with Augustine on many things, did not disagree on this point in any way, shape or form. It was he who said that, "A man who is a merchant can seldom if ever please God." These are harsh words. They refer to the fact that in Augustine's and Jerome's day, just like ours, people made money their god and lived for nothing else but acquiring more and more. Such people put their businesses as their ultimate concerns and took God out of the equation. They looked only to the world for their ultimate happiness. It is this that is being condemned.

Finally we have the great Church Doctor and orator for the faith, St. John Chrysostom, who said, "How did you become rich? Can you show the acquisition just? It cannot be. The root and origin of it must have been injustice." His experience was no different in how business people behaved in his day.

Some of the early Saints took great pains to forsake the entirety of the world. They lived in total deprivation of material goods in order to concentrate upon the beauty of God and to contemplate him as deeply as possible. Such a vocation is a rare one and not possible for all who even attempt it. Therefore, we need to point out there is a Christian way to do business that is based upon charity, fairness and morality. Such a business would be an ideal for any society to maintain to promote its general cultural health.

We see a change in just how the Christian culture operated around about the 1800s when the restriction imposed by the Biblically based early Christian communities went widely ignored. Thus began the present day downfall.

From the years of 1820 until 1970, there was a general trend in the US that attracted so many immigrants and gave citizens pride in their nation. The standard wage steadily rose and employers also provided the necessary tools to do the job more efficiently. The government also put in a set of regulatory laws that controlled the monster called "big business." Even during the depression that started in 1929, we still experienced a rise in wages. I want to also note that the depression went on from 1929 until

1945, the advent of World War II. The same procedures that were used to get out of the depression by the federal government then are the same as the ones used today. Why have we not learned from our past mistakes?

After World War II, prosperity here in America hit a peak. When we reached to 1970s, something happened to change all that. Wages suddenly began to dip and indeed never rose again. Employers also expected higher productivity from workers, despite the lack of raised wages. At the same time, advertising began to take an even more aggressive stance and emphasized how important consumerism was to live at a higher standard of living. It was at this point that big business started a new practice, it was called lending. Lending is great because the employer does not pay any additional wages and in lending you money, you have to pay him back...with interest! How great is that for the employer!?! So begins the raping, pillaging and demoralization of the American worker. Just look around you, every large corporation has in its portfolio some form of a lending institution such as a bank or a credit union. By the 1980s, we saw the fall and obliteration of Worker's Unions too. Big business tried to convince us all that it would be fair and impartial and uphold our rights. We had the wool pulled right over our eyes.

Recently, Unions have started once again to stand up and fight for worker's rights with the introduction of the "Right to Work" Bill. The name of this bill should be, "The Right to

Work for Less" Bill. This misnamed bill is a very nasty attempt by big business to stifle Unions and render them ineffective. It also tries to make people work for less money. How many times have we heard advocates for the rich say that there would be jobs for everyone if there was no minimum wage to hold companies back? This means we should work for a dollar a day while big business pulls in billions of dollars every year. Once again, it is stealing from the needy to give to the greedy.

Since the 1970s, the wealthiest 1% of the population in the US has seen its income tripled. They also account for 25% of all earned income in the US!! Why do they need a tax break? Studies have shown that the government stands to gain $800 billion just by properly taxing them. All of our problems would be gone.

I often ask myself how it is that so many Christians in big business, especially those who take the Bible literally, are able to freely justify their clearly sinful economic practices with a clear conscience. One wonders if the economic difficulties we experience (i.e. depressions, recessions, and inflations) are not deliberately manipulated into being to make some even richer than they are.

This having been said, a government based upon Christian ideals and values will implement the following:

Provide for the basic material necessities of those who cannot provide for themselves, such as the disabled and the elderly. This means a comprehensive social welfare system that responds to the needs of those who are truly deserving of help.

Allow people access to the necessary tools to earn a living. This would include free education. Logically, the next step would be to ensure job creation. This will allow citizens to fulfill the Biblical ideal that each person should be helped and guided to make themselves self-sufficient.

Finally, the government should allow for a class system to develop, only after the needs of the less fortunate have been met. Such a government should also enact laws and regulations to ensure that wealth was not gained through immoral and unethical means.

Is it against Biblical principles for a society to allow people to be wealthy? The answer is no. But to whom much is given, much is expected. To expound upon this fact, I recently read one of the ancient liturgies used by the Coptic Church. The liturgy traces itself back to about the year 400 A.D. In it, there is a litany which asks God to make the rich people be "good." In other words, to make them more Christ-like in their everyday behavior. I find it amazing that the more one acquires wealth, the more one wants, the more evil one becomes. It's a never ending circle. You get something and the satisfaction then goes away and then you want something else.

"How mistaken are the great majority of men! If they are rich, they at once desire honors; and if these are obtained, they are still unhappy; for never can that heart be satisfied which seeks anything but God."- St Therese the Little Flower

There also appears to be a correlation with increased levels of greed depending upon the more you have. It's like a drug. Dom Helder Câmara, the former archbishop of Recife in Brazil who recently died in 1999, was known as a defender of the poor and stated the following:

"I used to think when I was a child that Christ might have been exaggerating when He warned about the dangers of wealth. Today I know better. I know how very hard it is to be rich and still keep the milk of human kindness. Money has a dangerous way of putting scales on one's eyes, a dangerous way of freezing people's hands, eyes, lips, and hearts."

Wouldn't people be better off concentrating on the idea of being rather than having? Our fulfillment should come with the acquisition of knowledge and becoming more through our intellect to better mankind. Such actions would also bring about a sense of self-satisfaction. Are we not more God-like when we share our knowledge, our charity, and our love with others?

"But whoever has the world's goods, and beholds his brother in need and closes his heart against him, how does the love of God abide in him?" -1 John 3:17

Wages

"Do not take advantage of a hired man who is poor and needy, whether he is a brother Israelite or an alien living in one of your towns." -Deuteronomy 24:14

Colossians 4:1 issues a general command, urging masters to provide their slaves with what is "right and fair."

God's defense for those who are poor in Scripture seems to revolve around the practices of using dishonest scales, bribes, fraud, and physical violence against the poor. This is all in conjunction with taking what little property and belongings they already had.

James 5:1-6, which promises judgment on "rich oppressors," condemns them for failing to pay the workmen their wages. The emphasis, however, is not that the agreed wages were too low, but that the wages that were agreed on were not paid at all.

In an economic system where an employer is free to offer employees whatever wage he or she wishes above the minimum wage, the employer should really consider the amount of the wages he or she wishes to offer and decide if the wages would be fair and reasonable in the eyes of God. This is a moral obligation and not just a nice suggestion!

The Bible doesn't offer a guideline amount that a person should receive. The principle of being fair, realistic and, of course, loving your neighbor as yourself, can be the way to go in this situation. This concept does require that the employer has a conscience and can deal with empathy to his or her employees.

In looking at the past 100 years and the wages paid to the work force here in the US, it seems that the minimum wage kept going up until the 1970s. In the 1970s, we started to see a stagnation of wages. In fact, it seems as though they started to go down. Employers however demanded even more in the work load. So less people doing even more work and not getting paid enough to even survive. If we look at the percentages in 2011, the minimum wage had continued to increase as it was before the disaster of the 1970s, should now be between $14 and $17 an hour! This is a far cry from what people are making today.

I was reading about a Japanese concept called, "Karoshi." The term literally means, "death from overwork." It was coined a few decades back when a twenty-nine year old man who worked for a newspaper died of a stroke. The stress that drove his blood pressure sky high was in direct correlation to the psychological duress he received at work. His widow was able to prove this in a court of law and so the Japanese government awards, every year, compensation to those individuals or to those families who have suffered the ill effects of "Karoshi." How many victims of this do we see each year in the United States? This is not simply a disability concept, but rather, a punishment as well of those employers who inflict such horrible working conditions on their employees. The intended effect is to deter this from happening any further. This program has met with great success. This is all thanks to a government that thought about the welfare of its people first, not their financial elite.

Finally, on the subject of wages, let's take a look at the parable in which Jesus spoke of the workers in the vineyard and how they were chosen and paid.

"For the Kingdom of Heaven is like a man who was the master of a household, who went out early in the morning to hire laborers for his vineyard. When he had agreed with the laborers for a denarius a day, he sent them into his vineyard. He went out about the third hour, and saw others standing idle in the marketplace. To them he said, 'You also go into the vineyard, and whatever is right I will give you.' So they went their way. Again he went out about the sixth and the ninth hour, and did likewise. About the eleventh hour he went out, and found others standing idle. He said to them, 'Why do you stand here all day idle?' They said to him, 'Because no one has hired us.' He said to them, 'You also go into the vineyard, and you will receive whatever is right.' When evening had come, the lord of the vineyard said to his steward, 'Call the laborers and pay them their wages, beginning from the last to the first.' When those who were hired at about the eleventh hour came, they each received a denarius. When the first came, they supposed that they would receive more; and they likewise each received a denarius. When they received it, they murmured against the master of the household, saying, 'These last have spent one hour, and you have made them equal to us, who have borne the burden of the day and the scorching heat!' "But he answered one of them, 'Friend, I am doing you no wrong. Didn't you agree with me for a denarius? Take that which is yours, and go your way. It is my desire to give to this last just as much as to you. Isn't it lawful for me to do what I want to with what I own? Or is your eye evil, because I am good?' So the last will be first, and the first last. For many are called, but few are chosen." -Matthew 20:1-16

Many biblical scholars point to this parable as an allegory to the grace and mercy of God. I would say that there is also a practical message here as well. We know that the employer went to the usual place where the men would congregate hoping to get work for the day. It reminds me of a present day situation, where in some cities usually immigrants would congregate hoping to make an honest day's wage. So, all the men chosen had indeed waited there all day long.

The wage of a denarius was very generous indeed for any of the workers. We also know that the employer was equally generous to all. It was those who, despite being overpaid and working the hardest in the fields, still complained. They are reproved by the employer for their jealousy. Here Jesus is implying that we should not be petty and egotistical but rather work as a team and for the good of each member of the team. We are all equal as children of God. The workers who started early in the morning can be seen as the most "successful." How often do we see in our own lives that the successful often try to produce a culture that despises the "unsuccessful" or even better, the poor? God directly reproves this attitude.

We know that when one is unemployed, the finances tend to dwindle quickly. Each of those men, regardless of when they were chosen, still stood there ready, able and very willing to work. God's message here is that an employer has the obligation to provide for those in his employ. Namely, the worker has the right to a decent wage he can live on. There is also the implication here that we do need, as a society, to provide for the unemployed.

Clearly a denarius would be a day's wage, for example, for a soldier. It is quite generous to give this amount to a laborer. Yet here, Jesus tells us that employers must be generous. The employer, in being generous with his wages, implies that those who have wealth need to share with those who have fulfilled their end of the bargain. There is no implication here that those who were called did not work. All did the job they were called to do. The employee has the responsibility to provide a true and fair day of labor for his or her pay. The employer has the responsibility to not take advantage of those put into his or her care.

Second, the employer went out a few times to get more men. This implies that it is immoral for an employer to try to squeeze every last drop of blood and sweat from a small number of workers. This despicable practice can be seen so clearly today by employers who try to hire as few people as possible in order to maximize profits and outright abuse employees with truly sadistic performance goals.

I must confess that this parable gave me great difficulty in understanding until I really looked at it as a Christian should look at it. Can we deny the words of Christ or what He tries to convey to us through His words?

What Can We Do?

First and foremost, we need to re-examine our lives, our priorities, and our values. We must ask ourselves what we need to do to change what is happening around us. We can do it!

Jesus had a special sense of mission to the poor and oppressed people. At the outset of His ministry, sometimes referred to as Jesus' mission statement, Jesus stood up in the synagogue at Nazareth and read from the prophet Isaiah:

"The Spirit of the Lord is on me, because He has anointed me to preach good news to the poor. He has sent me to proclaim freedom for the prisoners and recovery of sight for the blind, to release the oppressed, to proclaim the year of the Lord's favor."-Luke 4:18-19

The biographies of Jesus depict him repeatedly reaching out to those at the bottom of the social pyramid—poor people, women, Samaritans, lepers, children, prostitutes and tax collectors. Jesus was also eager to accept people who were well-placed, but he made clear that all, regardless of social position, needed to repent. For this reason, He invited the rich young man to sell all of his possessions and give the proceeds to the poor (Matthew 19:16-30, Luke 18:18-30, Mark 10:17-31).

Jesus commanded, "love your neighbor." When asked to define "neighbor," Jesus expanded the traditional meaning of the word—defining our neighbor as anyone who is in need, including social outcasts: "But when you give a banquet, invite the poor, the crippled, the lame, the blind, and you will be blessed." -Luke 14:13

One by one's self can start change. One can be a catalyst for making the world right again. Feeling helpless is merely a temptation by the devil. We are powerful. We are strong and we can make a difference. Let us take a look at the story of David and Goliath (1 Samuel 17) and reflect for a moment on what it means to us in our lives today.

The Philistine army had gathered for war against Israel. The two armies faced each other, camped for battle on opposite sides of a steep valley. A Philistine giant measuring over nine feet tall and wearing full armor came out each day for forty days, mocking and challenging the Israelites to fight. His name was Goliath. Saul, the King of Israel, and the whole army were terrified of Goliath.

One day David, the youngest son of Jesse, was sent to the battle lines by his father to bring back news of his brothers. David was probably just a young teenager at the time. While there, David heard Goliath shouting his daily defiance and he saw the great fear stirred within the men of Israel. David responded, "Who is this uncircumcised Philistine that he should defy the armies of God?"

So David volunteered to fight Goliath. It took some convincing, but King Saul finally agreed to let David fight against the giant. Dressed in his simple tunic, carrying his shepherd's staff, slingshot and a pouch full of stones,

David approached Goliath. The giant cursed at him, hurling threats and insults.

David said to the Philistine, "You come against me with sword and spear and javelin, but I come against you in the name of the Lord Almighty, the God of the armies of Israel, whom you have defied [...] today I will give the carcasses of the Philistine army to the birds of the air [...] and the whole world will know that there is a God in Israel [...] it is not by sword or spear that the Lord saves; for the battle is the Lord's, and he will give all of you into our hands."

As Goliath moved in for the kill, David reached into his bag and slung one of his stones at Goliath's head. Finding a hole in the armor, the stone sank into the giant's forehead and he fell face down on the ground. David then took Goliath's sword, killed him and then cut off his head. When the Philistines saw that their hero was dead, they turned and ran. So the Israelites pursued, chasing and killing them and plundering their camp.

What can we say about this parable?

God has made each one of us special. Along with our unique identities, we have special gifts that were given to us by God. Just be yourself and use those gifts and talents God gave you. Allow yourself to be God's instrument and you will achieve miracles.

When we put things in proper perspective, we see more clearly and we can fight more effectively.

When the giant flexed his muscles, David didn't stop or waver. David did the right thing in spite of discouraging insults and fearful threats. Only doing what was right mattered to David.

David found some weaknesses in Goliath's armor. We too can look for weaknesses in our present system to topple down the tyranny that afflicts us. Our system was set up by human beings and is inherently imperfect, there are weaknesses in it and it will topple if pushed in the right place.

In this story we have the answers we need. We have God behind us for He has told us through the Bible what He wishes for our society. We also have His word on how the evil will all suffer.

"Come now, you rich, weep and howl for your miseries which are coming upon you. Your riches have rotted and your garments have become moth-eaten. [...] Behold, the pay of the laborers who mowed your fields and with you have withheld, cries out against you; and the outcry of the harvesters has reached the ears of the Lord of Sabaoth. You have lived luxuriously on the earth and led a life of wanton pleasure; you have fattened your hearts in a day of slaughter." -James 5:1-6.

Could the Bible be any clearer in its message? I think we need to go back to Aristotle, and remember that "the state or political community, which is the highest of all [communities], and which embraces all the rest, aims at good in a greater degree than any other, and at the highest good" (Politics 1.1).

As a Christian, I would take issue with this assertion that the political community is capable of attaining the highest good, it is actually the people of God (the Church) that can accomplish this. He brings up a point that is often forgotten: on the natural level, it is in the fair exercise of politics that humankind most gloriously shows forth the virtue, excellence and wisdom that humanity is capable of. It is one thing to be just and wise, but to diffuse justice and wisdom throughout the entire body politic is something marvelous. It is something which has never quite been done, though men from Plato to St. Thomas More ruminated upon it. But the essence of what I am getting at is that, abstractly speaking, politics is good and a forum for people to act with virtue and excellence. It is a far cry from today's government. This is where true democracy steps in and corrects everything! No Sheeple wanted here!

Democracy always works right when all people act righteously. The power truly is with the people. Look at that case in Florida where an innocent young man was killed just because another man perceived the young man as a threat. The older man perceived him as "menacing." So, he then shot and killed him. An outraged community stood up for its rights and the local officials took notice and were put into a position where they needed to re-examine the situation. Apparently the man who shot the young man was, originally, within his legal limits. He was definitely not within his moral limits and the people stood up and made a noise that could not be ignored. The murderer was then brought up on charges. These charges would not have resulted unless people united in one voice to say STOP the madness and give us justice!

We must remember that the local city council is a lot more influential in situations that affect our day to day lives so we need to be heard. The school board, the city council, the state representatives, and the local judiciary all touch the voter a lot more closely than the Senatorial or Presidential races. Yet who votes and does research on school board elections, whether the candidates are right for the job or not? Who turns out to vote for city councilmen, even though they decide whether the field behind your house stays a field or becomes a W-whatever supercenter? People need to make their voices heard! It is our right! It is our obligation!

In 2007, I traveled to England. While I was there, the BBC was broadcasting a story regarding Iceland. You see, Iceland had become the first nation to start the spiral downward financially into the great depression that we have all experienced. In 2008, they started to reach rock bottom.

In 2009, the Icelandic people en masse, went to parliament and started to pelt the building with stones against their leaders and the banks. They were demanding that the government leaders and the nation's bankers answer for the country's financial and economic collapse.

Because everyone banded together and demanded justice from the financial terrorism that the banks initiated, the banks were forced by the government and the people to forgive loans. In fact, the debt forgiveness was roughly equal to 13% of the gross national product!

Iceland took real and effective steps to resurrect itself. This is particularly amazing since the nation's banks had defaulted on approximately $85 billion! Yes! It's true; they got themselves out of the hole. Not by catering to the financial terrorists in the banking industry, but rather helping the people. So, by forgiving debt equal to 110% of the home values in the nation, they all prospered. Now they are considering putting the Prime Minister who was in charge at the time of the whole mess on trial. Good for them. They did it! They recovered and did so very nicely! And NO!, this is not a fairy tale but real life.

Here we have the perfect example to follow. The people of Iceland stood up to the jaws of financial terrorism and defeated it. They have now moved the country according to the will of the people and, thus, determined their own destiny. In 2012, the Icelandic government began to jail all those responsible for the financial crisis. Now they have gone after the true criminals for this tragedy. The banksters are paying for their greed. Why can they do it and wonderfully succeed while the rest of us can't do it here? It will work for us as well. Are we just once again being Sheeple? We just do not get involved nationally!

There is also an example of a government before WWII that had high unemployment, a stagnant economy, and was in a full-fledged depression. This all occurred during the same time that President Roosevelt was to implement the "New Deal." This European government also had the workers paying more in taxes than corporations and the rich. Does this sound familiar? This European government then did a total overhaul of its corrupt ways and totally reversed its financial and social well-being into a powerful nation.

It is my understanding that the first step was to lower the taxes on the workers and to substantially raise the taxes on the rich and corporations. Then the government limited the profits that corporations made to approximately 6%. It also limited the earnings from investments to the same percentage. Then the Government took the surplus money and invested it back into the country. It immediately created jobs and obliterated unemployment. It put in the proper social care and reform packages to help its citizens. It put everyone on the right track. It did not cater to financial terrorists but acted responsibly and helped its people. This is what a government is supposed to do. Conversely the "New Deal" instituted by Roosevelt, did not help to make a big turnaround. It helped a little and in the course of events, made a few of the wrong rich people even richer. I have heard the "New Deal" referred to as the "Raw Deal," and rightly so. The European government I described acted like a real democracy and not a plutonomy disguised as a democracy. The "New Deal" never pulled the nation out of its social and economic woes. What was the US government doing?

In 2012, the French people had a great advantage to take back their society and government. There were two choices for president. One was the incumbent who did not help the people and catered to the financial terrorists.

France, over the last five years, had grown much poorer and they were about to implement austerity measures. The other candidate had a different approach. This candidate proposed that the tax structure should be revamped. Those who make 150K to one million per year would pay 45% in taxes. Those who make over a million would have to pay 75% per year in taxes. He also proposed heavy measures against people and businesses that would attempt to take their earnings and profits outside of French jurisdiction. On Sunday May 6 2012, he won. The people voiced their opinion of how sick they were of the financial terrorism allowed by the old regime. The new guy got into office. A new day has dawned for France. In late 2012, the French government took on a new initiative. They started to tax the wealthy and businesses at 75%. This is definitely the step in the right direction for the well-being of the French people! Needless to say, the French economy is doing much better.

"The will of the people is the only legitimate foundation of any government, and to protect its free expression should be our first object."-Thomas Jefferson

These are choices the French people had to make. This is democracy in action. We must remember that democracies, at the end of the day, are governed bottom up; that is the only way anything can really change. The responsibility rests with us.

The Greeks as well have put a new government in. They too have suffered greatly under the grip of financial terrorism. They voted for only those parties that are "anti-bailout."

Hasn't that been the way with every sweeping revolution that has occurred? Look at the "Arab Spring" in the Middle East. All changes were brought about by the common persons who cared enough about their own situation and with their fellow people, made changes. Democracy means participation. We are all required to participate in this endeavor. We are also required to educate ourselves in how we should govern ourselves. Isn't it supposed to be "government for the people and by the people"? The minute we sit back and let things run themselves, or, do as little as possible, or, nothing at all, we have handed our rights over to those undeserving of such a privilege. We have become Sheeple.

America now looks exactly like the late Roman Republic. People had absolutely no confidence in local leaders and went to a few people in high places who actually operated above the law so they could get what they wanted. Look what happened to Rome. Rome became extremely corrupt. It destroyed itself slowly but surely. It ceased to be the rule of the people and became a dictatorship ruled by the Caesars. The people themselves caused this to happen because they did not take matters into their own hands. They became complacent, just like Sheeple. Do we want the same thing to happen to us? Do we want the 1% to rule us? We still have a chance to make a change, a real change, not some empty promise. It is not relying on one person or any one government. It is relying on ourselves.

"There is danger from all men. The only maxim of a free government ought to be to trust no man living with power to endanger the public liberty."-John Adams, Journal, 1772

If we do not make changes for ourselves, then let us think about our children. What kind of a world are we leaving them? Will we leave them a legacy of hope, or one of suffering? We have a responsibility also to God. We have the gift of His creation. We are all God's children and are part of His mystical body, that is, the Church here on earth. As God's children, we are one big family of brothers and sisters. Do we want to be dysfunctional? Or do we want to make everything right? We have the power to do it!!

"But understand this that in the last days there will come times of stress. For men will be lovers of self, lovers of money, proud, arrogant, abusive, disobedient to their parents, ungrateful, unholy, inhuman, implacable, slanderers, profligates, fierce, haters of good, treacherous, reckless, swollen with conceit, lovers of pleasure rather than lovers of God, holding the form of religion but denying the power of it. Avoid such people." -2 Timothy 3:1-5

This passage is just a little bit scary to me since it describes just how people in our society are acting today. We have a hard road ahead of us to make the world a better place. Are we in the last days? I don't know. The only real answer we can give is that God the Father has determined the date. Not even Jesus knows when. It is a good idea as St Paul says to live every day as though it were our last one. We are, after all, Christians first before all other identities. Heaven is our ultimate goal. Earth will pass away. Our time before God will be forever. Which is more important to you? That is the more important question.

If we learn to help one another and stop our ridiculous greed problems, we will be able to better the entire world. We will live as a people of God here on earth. We will ensure ourselves a place in Heaven in His glory for all eternity.

Everyone knows how an ostrich hides its head in the sand when danger approaches. It feels better with its quick fix making it blind to the world around it and not being able to hear the approaching consequences coming at it. Yet, despite the animal not hearing or seeing the danger, it still exists. In fact, such an approach is even more dangerous than standing up, evaluating, and then facing the problem.

Don't we need to restore sight, especially intellectual sight, to those who refuse to hear the truth? We may feel comfortable right now and so bury our heads in the sand. We may feel it's easier to remain as sheeple and not rock the boat. Then let me ask you, what kind of society are we handing down to our children? The sin of the matter is that our rights are being taken away from us, not because someone forces the issue, but because we relinquish them and we ignore the dire consequences of our lack of action.

Just remember, for evil to flourish, good men and women simply need to do nothing. By simply letting all that is bad for us happen, we are just as guilty as those who hurt humanity. Tell me, what choice will you make?